INVENTORS

INCREDIBLE STORIES of THE WORLD'S MOST INGENIOUS INVENTIONS

Written by Robert Winston

Illustrated by Jessamy Hawke

www.dk.com

CONTENTS

Caring for people

Making things go!

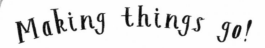

DK | Penguin Random House

Author Robert Winston
Illustrator Jessamy Hawke
Historical consultant Dr Stephen Haddelsey
Scientific consultant Lisa Burke

Editor Sally Beets
Designer Bettina Myklebust Stovne

Editorial Assistant Seeta Parmar
Design Assistant Katherine Marriott
Acquisitions Editor Sam Priddy
Senior Commissioning Designer Fiona Macdonald
Additional editorial Jolyon Goddard,
Katie Lawrence, Kathleen Teece
Additional design Jo Clark, Katie Knutton
Jacket Co-ordinator Issy Walsh
Senior Picture Researcher Sumedha Chopra
Managing Editors Laura Gilbert, Jonathan Melmoth
Managing Art Editor Diane Peyton Jones
Senior Production Editor Nikoleta Parasaki
Producer John Casey
Creative Directors Clare Baggaley, Helen Senior
Publishing Director Sarah Larter

Helping at home

Bang! Whizz! Whirr!

First published in Great Britain in 2020 by
Dorling Kindersley Limited
80 Strand, London, WC2R 0RL

Copyright © 2020 Dorling Kindersley Limited
Text copyright © Professor Robert Winston, 2020
A Penguin Random House Company
10 9 8 7 6 5 4 3 2 1
001–316658–May/2020

A CIP catalogue record for this book
is available from the British Library.
ISBN: 978-0-2414-1246-6

Printed and bound in China

A WORLD OF IDEAS:
SEE ALL THERE IS TO KNOW

www.dk.com

FOREWORD

by Professor Robert Winston

Human beings are very special because they are constantly inventing new things. We each have an exceptional ability — the ability to imagine. Unlike nearly all animals, we can make a picture of a machine, a tool, or a process in our brains that can help us to create something useful. Once we have had these thoughts, we can plan or draw them to find a way of making those ideas work. Some other really important skills are needed — one is persistence, and another is understanding that failure can be helpful. When our ideas fail to work, we can think about *why*, and then make improvements.

All inventors are persistent — constantly trying and trying again. All, at some point, experience failure but then improve what they have thought about or made. In this book, you will meet so many inventors that have changed the world, and others that have changed just the lives of those around them. However, each has contributed to human health or happiness, or improved things on this planet we inhabit.

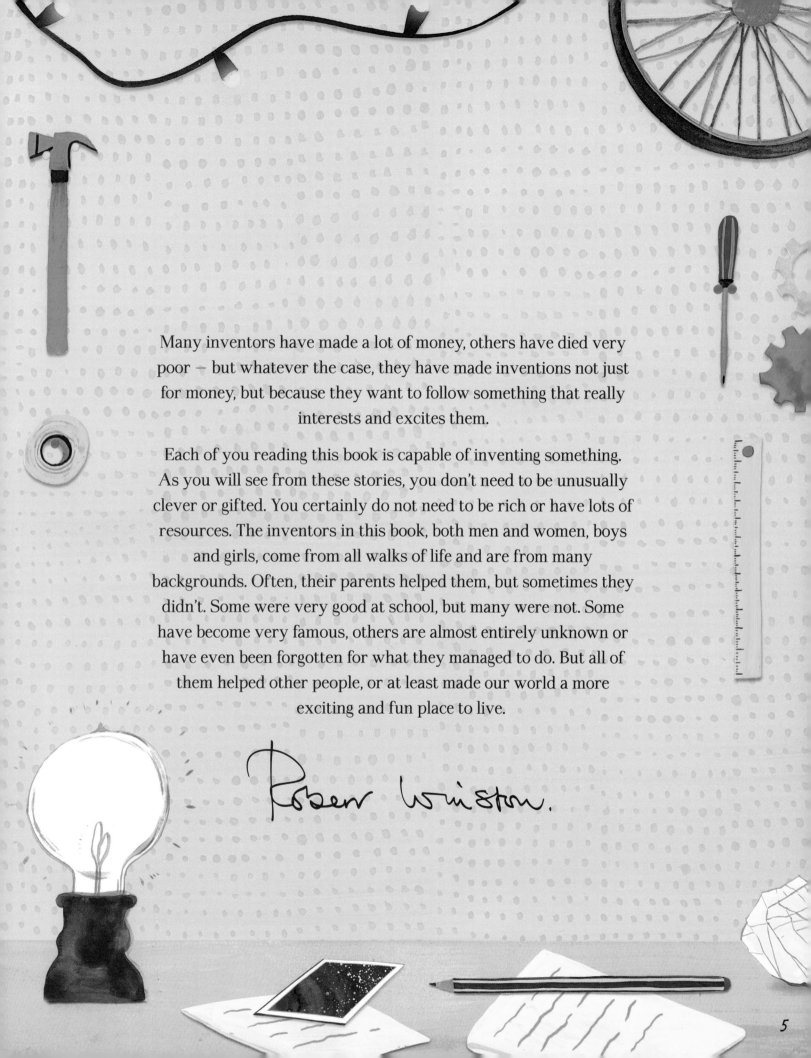

Many inventors have made a lot of money, others have died very poor – but whatever the case, they have made inventions not just for money, but because they want to follow something that really interests and excites them.

Each of you reading this book is capable of inventing something. As you will see from these stories, you don't need to be unusually clever or gifted. You certainly do not need to be rich or have lots of resources. The inventors in this book, both men and women, boys and girls, come from all walks of life and are from many backgrounds. Often, their parents helped them, but sometimes they didn't. Some were very good at school, but many were not. Some have become very famous, others are almost entirely unknown or have even been forgotten for what they managed to do. But all of them helped other people, or at least made our world a more exciting and fun place to live.

Robert Winston.

MAKING THINGS

GO!

Humans used to walk or use horses to travel around our world. As technology has become more advanced, inventors have come up with faster, and more ingenious ways to get around — be it on the ground, at sea, or in the sky.

LEONARDO DA VINCI

Italian inventor and artist
1452–1519

Leonardo da Vinci was one of the most brilliant minds in history. From his humble beginnings living on a farm with his mother, to moving in with his wealthy father at the age of five, Leonardo was always fascinated with both the beauty and mechanics of everyday objects.

Young Leonardo immersed himself in art. Aged 15, he began an apprenticeship alongside renowned artist Andrea del Verrocchioe in Florence, Italy, where he mastered painting and sculpting. However, this wasn't enough to quench his endless curiosity...

Leonardo studied birds and bats when designing his flying machines. The pilot would pedal to flap the wings.

Leonardo's painting The Mona Lisa *is unusual. Her eyes appear to follow you around!*

Mirror mastermind

To stop people from stealing his ideas, Leonardo developed an ingenious way of writing them down. By looking at the reflection of his writing in a mirror, Leonardo was able to write backwards! This meant that his notes were extremely hard to decode.

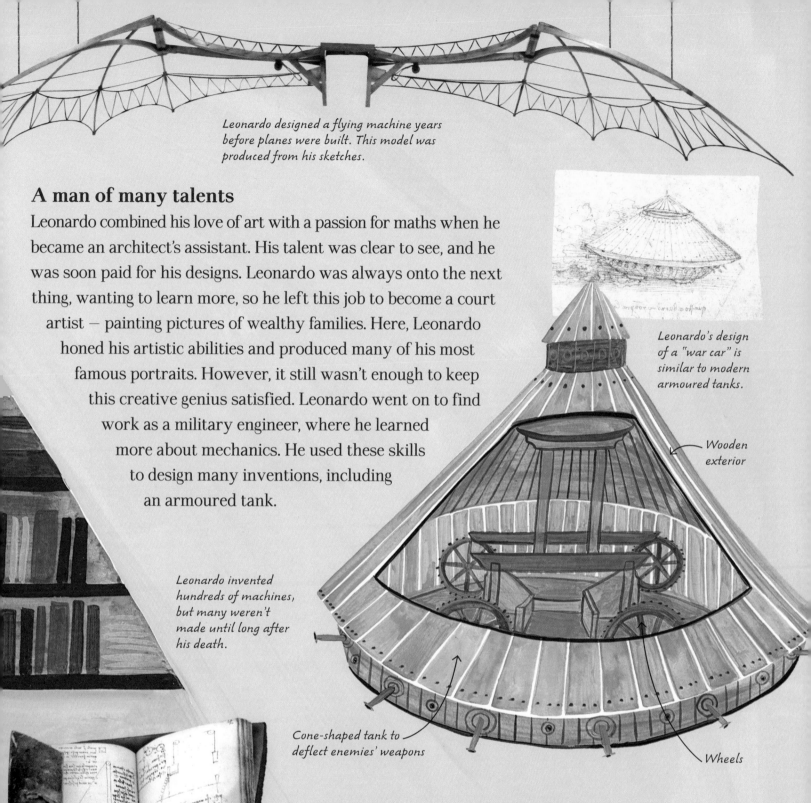

Leonardo designed a flying machine years before planes were built. This model was produced from his sketches.

A man of many talents

Leonardo combined his love of art with a passion for maths when he became an architect's assistant. His talent was clear to see, and he was soon paid for his designs. Leonardo was always onto the next thing, wanting to learn more, so he left this job to become a court artist — painting pictures of wealthy families. Here, Leonardo honed his artistic abilities and produced many of his most famous portraits. However, it still wasn't enough to keep this creative genius satisfied. Leonardo went on to find work as a military engineer, where he learned more about mechanics. He used these skills to design many inventions, including an armoured tank.

Leonardo's design of a "war car" is similar to modern armoured tanks.

Wooden exterior

Leonardo invented hundreds of machines, but many weren't made until long after his death.

Cone-shaped tank to deflect enemies' weapons

Wheels

Leonardo's notebooks contain many ideas for his inventions, such as a weapon for throwing stones called a bombard.

Flitting between art and mechanics throughout his life, Leonardo used the best parts of both disciplines for his inventions. His designs were years ahead of their time and are reflected in many objects we see today, such as the helicopter. Perhaps best known for painting *The Mona Lisa*, as well as his scientific, medical, and engineering drawings, Leonardo's incredible ideas live on.

THE WRIGHT BROTHERS

American aviation pioneers
Wilbur • 1867–1912
Orville • 1871–1948

Wilbur and Orville Wright had a dream, learned from failure, and persisted. Their interest in flight took off when, as boys, their dad bought them a toy helicopter. They always liked fiddling with machines and making things — when Orville was 12, he made kites that he sold to other children. In 1895, a famous mathematician and engineer called Lord Kelvin, stated that "heavier-than-air flying machines are impossible". But just eight years later, the Wright brothers flew the first aeroplane.

Wilbur and Orville began their careers by building their own printing press, but the two newspapers they published were not successful. When the bicycling craze hit the USA, they opened the Wright Cycle Company, selling and repairing bikes. However, the brothers were still fascinated by flight, and by a gliding pioneer called Otto Lilienthal.

The rudder turned the plane left and right.

How do aeroplanes fly?

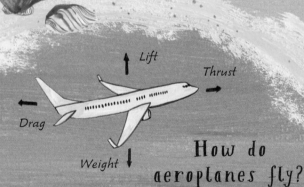

↑ Lift
→ Thrust
← Drag
↓ Weight

The plane's engine creates a forward force called thrust. As the plane moves forwards, air rushes over the wings to create another force — lift. For a plane to fly, thrust and lift must be stronger than the opposing forces of drag and weight.

Building a flying machine was their boyhood dream.

Is it a bird?

When they were constructing their plane, the brothers studied how birds fly. They noticed the way that birds tilt their wings to steer.

Getting it Wright

In 1896, Otto Lilienthal died in a gliding accident, but the Wright brothers were far from put off. Feeling sure that they could improve Otto's glider design, they set out to build their own. They created miniature wings (called airfoils) and tested these in a homemade wind tunnel. Then, they built a series of gliders and took turns flying them at Kitty Hawk, a beach in North Carolina, USA, where the sand allowed for a relatively soft landing.

By December 1903, the brothers felt ready to attempt a powered flight. They attached an engine and a rudder to the glider. First, Wilbur attempted to fly the aircraft, but the engine stalled on take-off. Three days later, on 17 December 1903, they tried again with Orville piloting — and it worked! The world's first powered flight lasted just 12 seconds, but it was the beginning of a new era. At 300 kg (660 lb), their flying machine was certainly heavier than air. The Wright brothers had achieved their dream, and changed the world forever.

The propeller spun to drive the plane forwards.

These flaps made the plane go up and down.

The pilot laid down on his stomach, next to the engine.

The first plane was called the Wright Flyer.

EARLY TRANSPORT

Many of us depend on transport to get to work and school every day. Yet, most of the modes of transport that we are familiar with today were only invented in the last few hundred years. These inventions changed our world forever.

The glider

British engineer Sir George Cayley (1773–1857) was the father of modern flight. His first glider took off carrying a 10-year-old – would you like to have been that child? Later, a servant was brave enough to fly in his larger glider. Unfortunately, it crashed.

The helicopter

Igor Sikorsky (1889–1972) was a Russian-American who invented the helicopter. He designed it in 1909, but it was 30 years until it was successfully built.

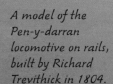

A model of the Pen-y-darran locomotive on rails, built by Richard Trevithick in 1804.

The penny farthing

This early bicycle got its name after the old British penny and farthing coins, as one was much larger than the other. The penny farthing was built by James Starley (1830–1881) in about 1870. The large front wheel made it possible to go fast and also acted as a shock absorber.

The jet plane

German Hans von Ohain (1911–1998) created the jet engine in 1937. It powered the Heinkel He 178 in 1939 but the plane was very difficult to fly. The Englishman Sir Frank Whittle (1907–1996) was working on a similar engine at the same time – also firing it up in 1937.

The Heinkel He 178

Powered flight

Some people think Brazilian Alberto Santos-Dumont (1873–1932) flew the first powered airplane as the Wright brothers used a launching rail to help take off. Alberto flew his winged aircraft over Paris in 1906, amazing the crowds. He survived many crashes.

The Gross-Lichterfelde Tramway opened in 1881, in Berlin, Germany.

The steam-powered locomotive

Richard Trevithick (1771–1833) built the first steam locomotive, which ran up a hill in Cornwall, UK, in about 1800. The steering wasn't brilliant and it crashed. He then engineered later steam engines that ran on rails.

Electric tram

Trams run along the street on rails. The first electric tram railway was established in St Petersburg, Russia, by Fyodor Pirotsky in 1880. Werner von Siemens talked to Fyodor when he built his more successful line in Berlin, Germany, in 1881.

FERDINAND VON ZEPPELIN

German general and inventor
1838–1917

During World War I, a terrifying floating figure haunted Britain's night skies. This was the zeppelin, named after its creator, Count Ferdinand von Zeppelin.

Growing up, Ferdinand lived with his wealthy family in a manor house near Lake Constance in Germany. When he was 17, he went to military school and within three years became an officer in the army. In 1863, the army sent him to observe the American Civil War. While staying in Minnesota, USA, Ferdinand met the famous aeronaut (hot-air balloon pilot) John Steiner, who took him on his first balloon ride. Ferdinand returned to Germany in 1866, where he began to ponder the military potential of airships.

In 1910, Ferdinand launched the first aircraft service for passengers.

Getting it off the ground

After leaving the army, Ferdinand dedicated himself
to developing a new type of airship. In 1895, he patented his design — a rigid,
cigar-shaped aircraft 170 m (558 ft) in length, driven by propellers, and containing
several balloons filled with hydrogen, a lighter-than-air gas. The next
challenge was figuring out how to fly it safely.

The first flight took place over Lake Constance in 1900, but the craft
was badly damaged on landing. Out of money, Ferdinand needed the help of the king of
Württemberg, a region of Germany, to pay for further trials. After six years, the second
zeppelin flew, but had to land soon after due to engine failure. Finally, in 1906,
Ferdinand produced a successful airship — the *Zeppelin LZ 3*. Despite an accident
in 1908 when an airship caught fire, Ferdinand's invention had captured
the public's imagination, and he was able to start a company producing zeppelins.

The popularity of Ferdinand's airships soared, and by 1914, more than
34,000 people across Germany had travelled on one. The army became interested,
and zeppelins were modified to bomb enemy countries during World War I. They were a
terrifying sight, but not as effective as the Germans had hoped. The bombs often missed
their targets, and zeppelins were huge, slow-moving and highly flammable, so they were
easy to shoot down. Sadly, Ferdinand died in 1917, so never saw his airships cross the
Atlantic, or travel around the globe in 1929.

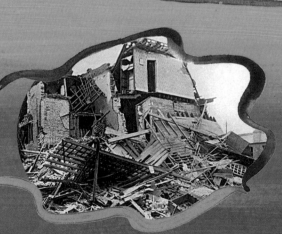

More than 500 British people were
killed by zeppelins from 1915 to 1918,
and many buildings were destroyed.

After the war,
Germany built more
zeppelins, including
the Graf Zeppelin,
which made the
first-ever passenger
flight across the
Atlantic in 1928.

Karl Benz loved speed — and eventually went faster than anybody had before. His father died when Karl was two, leaving the family with little money. Karl's mother made sure that he went to a good school and university. He did various jobs rather unsuccessfully — metalworking, making locks, designing bridges — but his dream was to create an engine powerful enough to drive carriages.

Bertha drove the first car. During her trip, she stopped to buy leather from a shoemaker and attached it to the brake blocks — like modern-day brake pads.

Karl married a rich woman named Bertha Ringer, and with her financial help his dream to build engines came true. These engines powered the so-called "horseless carriage" that he built, which looked like a tricycle. It was the birth of the first-ever car, though it couldn't go quite as fast as a horse-drawn carriage — with a top speed of roughly 13 kph (8 mph). Karl and Bertha loved the noisy sound of the engine, but others found it frightening — it was even called the "devil's carriage" by the church. Bertha, however, didn't give up. She thought that all her husband's invention needed for success was a little publicity...

Karl acquired a patent for his Motorwagen car in 1886. The word "car" comes from the word "carriage".

In 1926, Benz's company merged with another to form Daimler-Benz, which still produces Mercedes-Benz cars today.

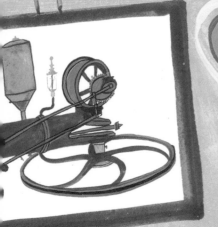

Bob Burman drove the *Blitzen Benz* in 1911, breaking records.

Bertha's daring drive

One day in 1888, without telling Karl, Bertha took their sons Eugen and Richard, in the horseless carriage to visit their grandmother, who lived 120 km (75 miles) away. The car gained a lot of attention — some people wanted to test-drive it, others thought it was a "smoking monster"! Happily, they arrived safe and sound. It was the world's first-ever long-distance drive.

Bertha noted that the vehicle needed another gear to help it climb hills, and also better brakes. Much improved, Karl's automobiles were soon famous, and by 1899 his factory had made nearly 600 of them. In 1909, Karl built the *Blitzen Benz*, a bullet-shaped single-seater car that went more than 225 kph (140 mph). People who drove it said it bumped up and down so much their eyeballs rattled in their sockets! It remained the fastest car in the world until 1920. Today, Karl and Bertha are seen as a driving force behind modern cars.

Karl developed the first petrol engine that would eventually power the first cars.

KARL & BERTHA BENZ
German mechanical engineer • 1844–1929
German car pioneer • 1849–1944

KÄTHE PAULUS

German aerial performer
1868–1935

It takes a lot of guts to parachute from a great height. It also takes a parachute that unfolds properly. At a time when people had previously failed to get these devices to open out from backpacks, Käthe Paulus invented a new type, which actually worked.

Before flying high in the sky, Käthe had chosen the grounded life of a seamstress. Everything changed when she met the man she would go on to marry, the hot air balloonist and parachutist Hermann Lattemann. He transfixed her with his tales of performing aerial tricks in the sky, so she set down her needle and joined him as an assistant. Her skills as a seamstress could now be put to use creating and mending balloons.

Not content with just sewing the balloons, Käthe ascended in one for her first parachute jump in 1893. The airship reached 1,200 m (3,900 ft), and she became the first woman in Germany, and the third woman in history, to take the leap.

Käthe's shows were famous across Germany.

The folding parachute

Käthe's parachute could be folded into a pack and worn on the back, to be released during a jump. It then unfolded in the air above the parachutist. It was tricky to prevent the lines — which attached the parachute to the parachutist — from getting twisted and tangled. Käthe created an ingenious way of arranging the lines and folding the parachute.

One-woman show

Käthe became a popular part of Hermann's aerial shows. However, these came to a sudden halt when Hermann fell to his death because his parachute didn't open properly during a performance. Käthe was devastated. However, helped by fan letters celebrating her achievements, she once more began to tour, using her performance name of "Miss Polly".

The German army realized the parachute design could save lives, and soldiers used them to land safely.

She became a one-woman act that drew crowds of thousands. "Miss Polly" would swing from bars beneath balloons high in the air, and even rode across the sky on a bicycle attached to a giant balloon called a blimp. But Käthe knew she could do even more breathtaking stunts if she could perfect a parachute that unfolded from a backpack. This would allow her to fall for longer as she could release the parachute mid-jump.

From seamstress to star performer of the sky.

After working hard for many years, Käthe managed to create such a parachute. She patented it in 1915, and when the German army heard about the device they soon ordered 7,000 for their troops, who were fighting in World War I. Balloonists sent to keep watch from the skies could stow Käthe's parachutes in their balloons and use them to jump to safety if the balloons were shot down. In 1917, Käthe received a war medal from Germany — the Cross of Merit for War Aid — because her invention had saved multiple lives.

Now parachutists always carry a parachute on their backs, just like Käthe.

G. D. NAIDU
Indian engineer and inventor
1893–1974

He didn't receive much of an education, but Gopalswamy Naidu, also known as G. D. Naidu, taught himself how to build machines – and invented a great many of his own. There are tales of Gopalswamy throwing mud at his teachers because he disliked primary school so much, and he certainly didn't make it to secondary school. Instead, he began working on his family's farm. He might have spent the rest of his life there if it weren't for a chance encounter with a motorbike.

Gopalswamy had never seen a motorbike before when one broke down near his farm. He was so excited by the idea of motorised transport that he walked 26 km (16 miles) from his village in southern India to the city of Coimbatore to try to buy a vehicle for himself. He didn't have enough money, so worked long hours as a hotel waiter to save up. Finally, he was able to buy his own motorbike.

Electric motor

In 1937, Gopalswamy designed the first electric motor ever to be made in India. It was produced by his company, the National Electric Works.

Gopalswamy taught himself the basics of engineering by taking his motorbike apart and figuring out how it worked.

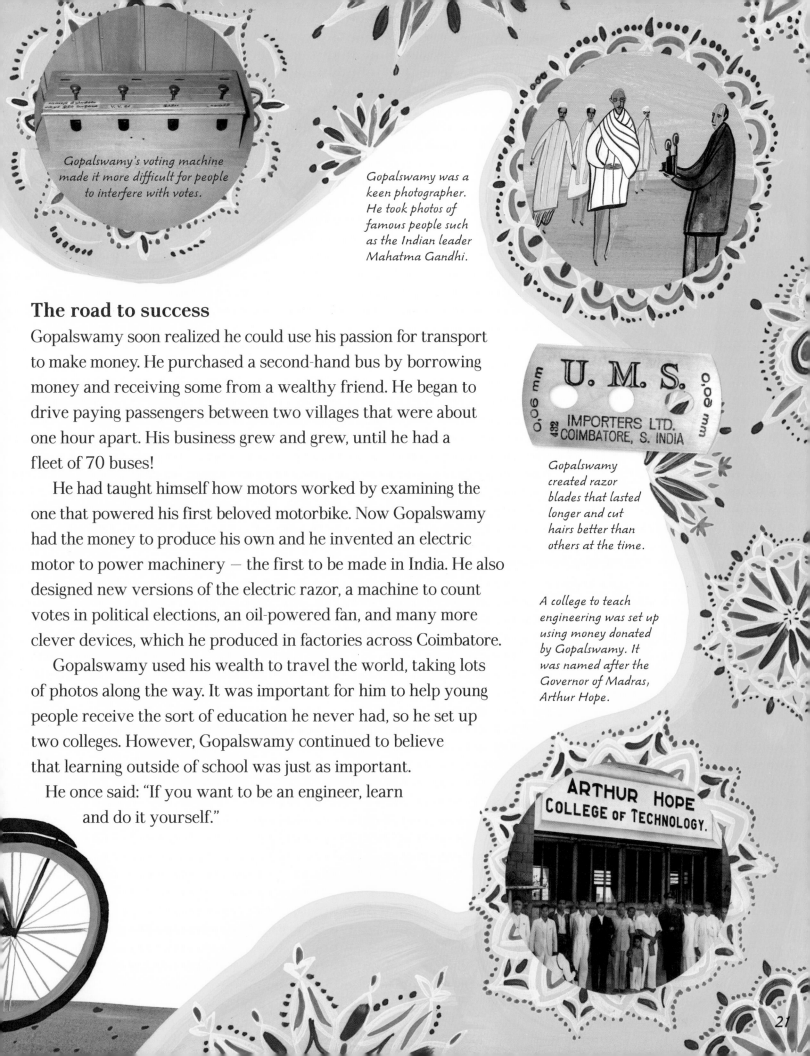

Gopalswamy's voting machine made it more difficult for people to interfere with votes.

Gopalswamy was a keen photographer. He took photos of famous people such as the Indian leader Mahatma Gandhi.

The road to success

Gopalswamy soon realized he could use his passion for transport to make money. He purchased a second-hand bus by borrowing money and receiving some from a wealthy friend. He began to drive paying passengers between two villages that were about one hour apart. His business grew and grew, until he had a fleet of 70 buses!

He had taught himself how motors worked by examining the one that powered his first beloved motorbike. Now Gopalswamy had the money to produce his own and he invented an electric motor to power machinery — the first to be made in India. He also designed new versions of the electric razor, a machine to count votes in political elections, an oil-powered fan, and many more clever devices, which he produced in factories across Coimbatore.

Gopalswamy used his wealth to travel the world, taking lots of photos along the way. It was important for him to help young people receive the sort of education he never had, so he set up two colleges. However, Gopalswamy continued to believe that learning outside of school was just as important.

He once said: "If you want to be an engineer, learn and do it yourself."

U.M.S. IMPORTERS LTD. COIMBATORE, S. INDIA

Gopalswamy created razor blades that lasted longer and cut hairs better than others at the time.

A college to teach engineering was set up using money donated by Gopalswamy. It was named after the Governor of Madras, Arthur Hope.

ARTHUR HOPE COLLEGE OF TECHNOLOGY.

HIDEO SHIMA

Japanese engineer
1901–1998

The rails are joined together in one large piece, so the trains run smoothly.

Each car has an individual electric motor.

Hideo inherited his passion for railways from his father. Yasujiro Shima was a brilliant railway engineer who first proposed the idea of the *dangan ressha* ("bullet train") that would zip across Japan at impossibly high speeds. Sadly, Yasujiro died before he could see his dream become a reality. However, his son would go on to build the fastest train in the world.

After studying mechanical engineering at university, Hideo started working for the Japanese government in 1925, designing steam locomotives (the vehicles that power the trains). During this time he came up with an important idea. Hideo thought that trains could be powered by electric motors attached to each car, rather than by one big engine at the front.

JAPAN

Tokyo

Osaka

The Tokaido Shinkansen
The Tokaido Shinkansen runs for 500 km (300 miles) between Tokyo and Osaka. By 1965, a year after it was launched, the Shinkansen took only 3 hours and 10 minutes to reach the city of Osaka from Tokyo, twice as fast as other trains.

Hideo designed the aerodynamic nose.   *Overhead electric power supply*

The Shinkansen

Hideo and his team made the Shinkansen faster and safer than any train before. He was modest about his role and said that he simply brought together advances in existing technology using the creativity of everyone involved.

Speeding up

In 1955, Hideo became Chief Engineer on the Shinkansen ("new trunk line") project, in charge of building the first high-speed electric train line in the world. It was the first train to reach speeds of more than 209 kph (130 mph). Bullet trains had a huge impact on Japanese society — more people travelled to the cities to work, and businesses boomed. Despite its success, Hideo remained humble. He was hard on himself, and felt that he had to resign as the project cost so much money.

Hideo's original line, the Tokaido Shinkansen, still holds an unmatched safety record of zero fatal accidents. Despite running more than 300 trains a day, it remains famous for always arriving on time.

On 1 October 1964, the first bullet train left Tokyo Station. Hideo was sadly not invited to the opening ceremony as he left the project in 1963.

HEDY LAMARR
Austrian–American actor
1914–2000

Hedy Lamarr was a Hollywood actor whose actual life story was even more amazing than a movie. Known as "the most beautiful woman", she was typically cast in glamorous roles that had few lines. However, the real Hedy was as brainy as she was beautiful, and had hidden, inventive talents.

From movie star...

Born Hedwig Eva Kiesler in Austria, she was a teenager when she dropped out of school to become an actor. After starring in a few European films, Hedwig was convinced by the head of a major film company that changing her name would help her break into Hollywood. And so, Hedy Lamarr was born. Hedy's fame grew as she starred in one box-office hit after another, however, she often felt lonely and homesick. There was one thing that cheered her up, though, and in between takes she concentrated on her true passion — inventing

Hedy starred in more than 30 films, opposite famous Hollywood actors such as Clark Gable.

All creative people want to do the unexpected.

Hedy suggested that Howard Hughes, a famous businessman and pilot, change the square design of his planes to make them more streamlined, like birds.

Wi-Fi pioneer

From streamlining planes, to creating a tablet that made drinks fizzy (but also taste horrible), some of Hedy's ideas and inventions were better than others. Her greatest triumph, however, changed the way we communicate forever. She discovered that torpedoes — weapons controlled using radio signals during World War II — could easily be intercepted to stop them from reaching their target. She teamed up with a friend, the composer George Antheil, to develop a way of coding the signals to avoid this happening, called "frequency-hopping spread spectrum" technology. This was later used by the US Navy and developed into technology we use every day, such as talking on mobile phones and using Wi-Fi.

...to inventor extraordinaire!

In 1997, Hedy was finally given an award for her pioneering inventions.

Hedy wanted to join the National Inventors Council — a US organization that developed inventions with military uses — but was told that she would be more helpful if she used her celebrity status to get people to donate to the war. As a beautiful film actor, Hedy didn't fit the part of the scientist — people just couldn't accept that she could be glamorous as well as a brilliant inventor. As she said, during the one interview where she spoke about her interest in inventing, her story is truly "the opposite of what people think".

MARY SHERMAN MORGAN

American rocket scientist
1921–2004

As a little girl, Mary's only toy was a doll made of dried leaves from an ear of corn.

Mary's family burned lignite (toxic coal) to keep warm, sparking her interest in chemistry.

Mary was a rocket scientist who made possible the launch of the USA's first satellite into space. Her early life, however, was very down to earth. Mary was raised on a run-down farm in a small community of 300 people in North Dakota, USA. When she was eight, social services visited her home as Mary wasn't attending school. This was because her father expected her to help on the farm, doing chores such as milking the family cow, Irma. But once she started going to school, Mary did very well.

Mary didn't want to live on the farm for the rest of her life so when she was old enough, she left for university. Soon afterwards, World War II broke out and many men joined the army. With the shortage of male workers, Mary was offered a job at a factory in Ohio. However, this was no ordinary factory — it made explosives for the war.

From farmer's daughter...

Caption: Explorer 1 satellite in orbit. It was just over 2 m (6.5 ft) in length.

Launching her career

After the war, the USA and the Soviet Union began competing in the Space Race — a race to be the first nation to send human-made objects into space. Mary was offered a job at North American Aviation, where they made rocket fuel. Among 900 engineers, Mary was the only woman, and one of the very few without a university degree. In 1957, the Russians launched a satellite called *Sputnik 1* into orbit. The Americans couldn't launch their own satellite as their fuel did not produce enough thrust for rockets to escape Earth's gravity. Mary was put in charge of finding a new fuel that would work. After weeks of doing complex mathematical calculations, Mary and her team cracked the problem and developed a new liquid fuel called hydyne.

The USA successfully launched its first satellite, *Explorer 1*, in 1958. Mary's top-secret work had saved the US space programme. Incredibly, even Mary's own children didn't know how important their mother's work had been until after her death. Mary never talked about her past, but her story is finally being told — inspiring future female scientists around the world.

Caption: Millions of women worked at explosives factories during World War II. It was tough and dangerous work, and injuries were common.

Caption: The Juno 1 rocket was used to launch Explorer 1.

...to rocket scientist

Caption: Against her parents' wishes, Mary left for university to study chemistry. However, she did not graduate.

The Space Race

During the 1950s and 1960s, the USA and the Soviet Union accomplished amazing feats in space flight. The Russians sent the first man into space in 1961. Eight years later, an American astronaut crew landed on the Moon.

NAVIGATING THE SEAS

Sea-gazing inventors realized that the only way to explore the vast oceans was by creating vehicles to take people out there. They dreamed up boats that could cover long distances and submarines to take people into the deep. Other inventions helped sailors find the right route, when there was nothing but water for hundreds of miles around.

Compass

The compass was invented in China around 2,000 years ago. It always points to the Earth's magnetic North Pole, so people can use it to find their way.

Astrolabe

The astrolabe was invented thousands of years ago by an unknown genius. Sailors could use it to find the angle of the Sun or stars from the ground and then work out how far north or south their ship was from the equator, which is an invisible line around the centre of the Earth.

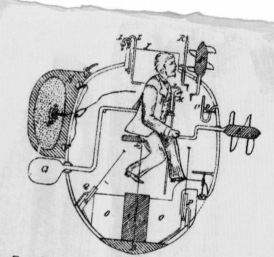

David's one-person vessel, built in 1775, used hand-turned propellers to move through water.

Submarine

Submarines take people deep down beneath the surface of the ocean. Perhaps the most successful early submarine was David Bushnell's, which was used to allow American soldiers to attach bombs to British warships during the American Revolution.

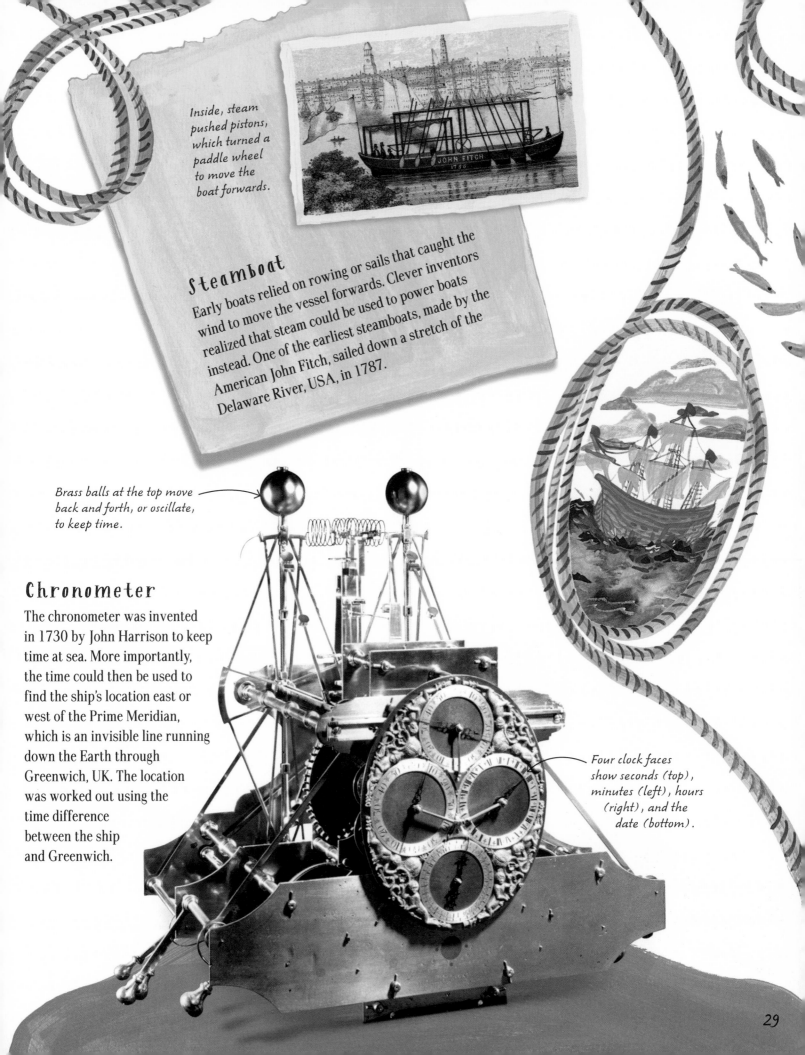

Inside, steam pushed pistons, which turned a paddle wheel to move the boat forwards.

Steamboat

Early boats relied on rowing or sails that caught the wind to move the vessel forwards. Clever inventors realized that steam could be used to power boats instead. One of the earliest steamboats, made by the American John Fitch, sailed down a stretch of the Delaware River, USA, in 1787.

Brass balls at the top move back and forth, or oscillate, to keep time.

Chronometer

The chronometer was invented in 1730 by John Harrison to keep time at sea. More importantly, the time could then be used to find the ship's location east or west of the Prime Meridian, which is an invisible line running down the Earth through Greenwich, UK. The location was worked out using the time difference between the ship and Greenwich.

Four clock faces show seconds (top), minutes (left), hours (right), and the date (bottom).

CARING
FOR PEOPLE

Meet the inventors who care for our world. Some of them have developed a cure for a disease or created a tool to help people communicate, while others have come up with innovative tools for recycling or for purifying water. These compassionate creations have improved the lives of people around the world.

SEJONG THE GREAT

Korean king • 1397–1450

Many kings are called "Great", but few change their country's written language in the way that King Sejong did. As a boy, he was more gifted and intelligent than his two elder brothers. One of his brothers, Yangnyeong, was removed as king because of bad behaviour, while the other, Hyoryeong, became a monk. Sejong was named as king when he was 22 years old. He was to become a wise and powerful ruler.

Fascinated by poetry and stories, Sejong was passionate about promoting Korean literacy. At that time, Koreans did not have their own language. Instead, thousands of complex Chinese symbols were used — which made it difficult for ordinary people to learn to read and write. Sejong invented the alphabet Hangul, made up of a shorter alphabet of 28 letters. Sejong saw books as a means to spread education among his people. The effects are felt to this day, as Korea has high rates of literacy.

This sundial was created by Jang Yeong-Sil, who Sejong employed as an inventor.

A man ahead of his time

Sejong gave money to inventors to explore science. The most famous was a man called Jang Yeong-sil, who designed water clocks, sundials, a sphere showing the movement of planets, and a rain gauge.

King Sejong was quite modern in his thinking and many of his rulings were controversial. He shocked some by appointing people from different social classes into important positions. Many of his experts, including Jang the inventor, came from poorer backgrounds. He also made laws that gave new parents time off work after they had babies, and distributed food to people who could not afford it.

Sadly for a man who loved books and reading so much, Sejong went blind in middle age and died a few years later. King Sejong's period of rule became known as the "Golden Age" of Korea because of the many advances that took place.

This book, called the Hunminjeongeum, described how Hangul worked. It was written in Chinese.

How Hangul works

The Korean alphabet, known as Hangul in South Korea, and *Chosôn muntcha* in North Korea, has changed very little since King Sejong invented it. Each letter has its own distinct sound and the consonants look like the shape of the mouth when speaking them. Letters are arranged in two-level blocks.

In Hangul, the word "invention" is:

b   a   m   yeo

빌 명

l   ng

Pronounced:

"bal myeong"

Sejong remains an important figure in South Korea and is shown on their 10,000 won note.

LOUIS BRAILLE
French educator
1809–1852

This line of Braille spells Louis' name.

Louis Braille had a horrible accident when he was three years old, which ended up changing the lives of millions of people. He lived with his family in Coupvray, a village noted for excellent cheese-making, about 40 km (25 m) from Paris. Next to their cosy living room, Louis' dad repaired saddles in his workshop and Louis loved to watch him work. One day, when nobody was about, Louis picked up a sharp tool to make holes in some leather himself, but his hands were too little, and the tool slipped, entering his eye. Louis' eye got infected and he couldn't see out of it, then gradually his other eye also got infected. By the time he was five, Louis was completely blind.

Louis enjoyed playing in his dad's leather workshop.

Louis, in an odd way, was lucky. When he was 10 he entered the Royal Institute for Blind Youth in Paris, winning many prizes. The school's founder, Valentin Haüy, taught the children to read by touching letters that stood out on the paper. When he was 11, Louis met Captain Barbier, a visiting army officer. He'd invented a reading system that used dots and lines that could be felt. This invention meant his troops could read simple messages in pitch darkness.

The Royal Institute for Blind Youth in Paris was the first school for blind children in the world.

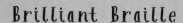

Louis held the position of organist in the Church of Saint-Nicolas-des-Champs, Paris, between 1834 and 1839.

Six dots

Captain Barbier's system was slow, complex, and couldn't spell sentences. Louis wanted to create a proper alphabet for blind people to use so that they could read and write individual words. By the age of 16, this child genius had created his own system — now known as "Braille" — using different combinations of six dots to represent letters of the alphabet. But he did not stop there. Louis was musical — an accomplished organist — and his system included musical notes as well as numbers and punctuation. Louis became a tutor at his old school and his system gradually became famous. He had to give up teaching when he became ill with tuberculosis. Thereafter, he spent more and more time in that cosy living room in Coupvray, until he died aged 43.

Brilliant Braille

The Braille system uses dots to represent letters. Louis reduced Captain Barbier's reading system from 12 dots to 6, and created 63 different combinations of them, each in a space no larger than a fingertip. The system is now used by visually impaired people across the world.

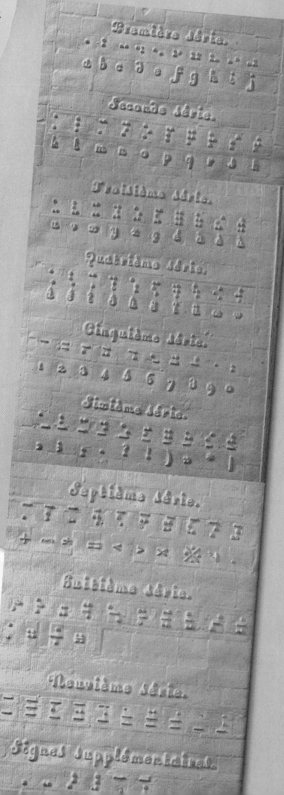

The Braille version of Harry Potter and the Deathly Hallows was released the same day as the print version. It is more than 1,000 pages long.

The world is divided into 24 time zones, each an hour apart, marked by invisible lines.

In 1851, Sandford designed the Threepenny Beaver, the first Canadian postage stamp.

Sandford's proposed route

Vancouver

Final route

Ontario

Sandford helped build the Canadian Pacific Railway.

The central time zone runs through Greenwich, UK.

Sandford Fleming **once missed a train** and became determined that it never happen again. He created a system that would improve not just his own timekeeping, but would help people around the world too.

Sandford left school at 14 to become an apprentice map-maker. When he was 18, he moved from Scotland to Canada. In 1851, he created a scientific organization with some friends, called the Royal Canadian Institute.

Sandford was a tough man who loved the open air and spent years surveying land for the government, which was planning to construct a new railway. He designed and built much of it but was sacked before it was finished. Sandford was heartbroken, but he would bounce back.

Sandford, in the tallest hat, witnessed the last spike being driven into the Canadian Pacific Railway.

SANDFORD FLEMING
Scottish-Canadian engineer
1827–1915

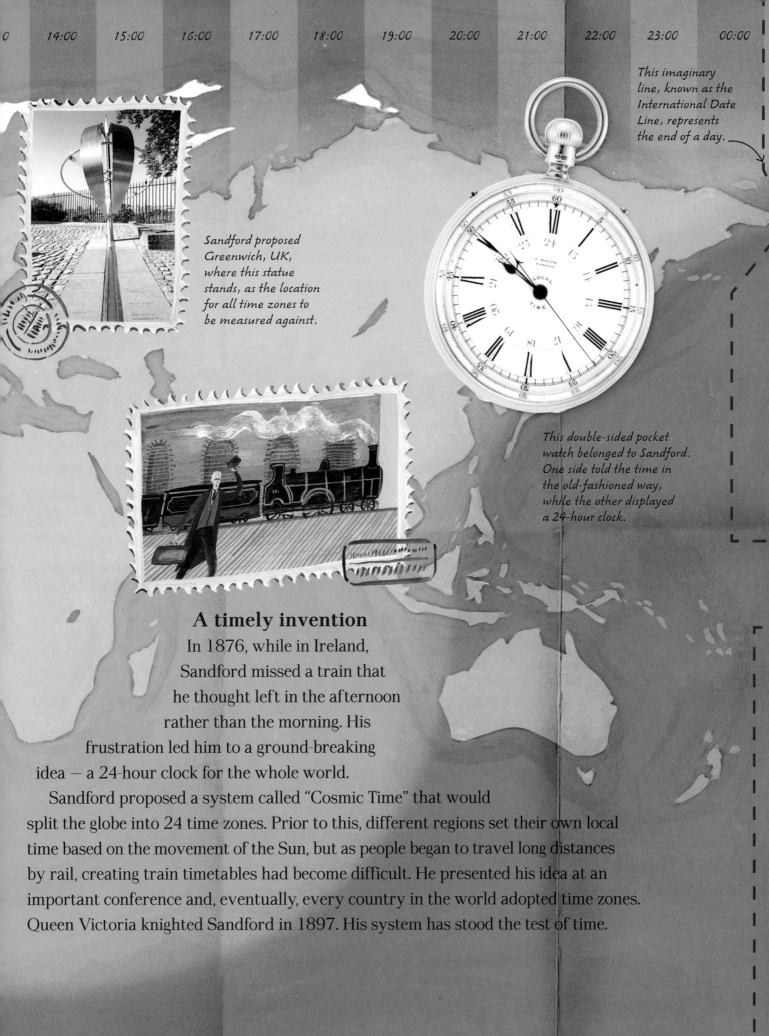

This imaginary line, known as the International Date Line, represents the end of a day.

Sandford proposed Greenwich, UK, where this statue stands, as the location for all time zones to be measured against.

This double-sided pocket watch belonged to Sandford. One side told the time in the old-fashioned way, while the other displayed a 24-hour clock.

A timely invention

In 1876, while in Ireland, Sandford missed a train that he thought left in the afternoon rather than the morning. His frustration led him to a ground-breaking idea — a 24-hour clock for the whole world.

Sandford proposed a system called "Cosmic Time" that would split the globe into 24 time zones. Prior to this, different regions set their own local time based on the movement of the Sun, but as people began to travel long distances by rail, creating train timetables had become difficult. He presented his idea at an important conference and, eventually, every country in the world adopted time zones. Queen Victoria knighted Sandford in 1897. His system has stood the test of time.

WILHELM CONRAD RÖNTGEN

German mechanical engineer and physicist • 1845–1923

Wilhelm Conrad Röntgen didn't finish school, but he still made one of the most important discoveries in medicine, ever. In 1866, Wilhelm met his future wife, Anna, in her father's café. Wilhelm's dad didn't approve of the match as he didn't think Anna was wealthy enough – but the two married anyway. Anna would end up becoming part of history as the subject of a very famous photograph.

Wilhelm managed to go to university despite leaving school early, and afterwards began studying radiation – rays given off by some materials. In 1885, he discovered X-rays when passing high-voltage electricity through a glass tube. He found that the rays passed through skin but they did not penetrate lead or bones. To demonstrate this phenomenon, Wilhelm took an X-ray photograph of Anna's hand. She saw her bones and gasped: "I have seen my death!"

The X-rays bounced off Anna's bones and ring, which showed on the photograph.

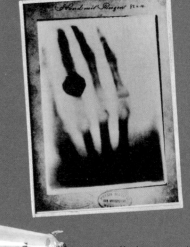

Wilhelm noticed the X-rays from the glass tube when they made a nearby screen glow.

Wilhelm held things in front of the X-rays to see which of them the rays could pass through, including his own hand!

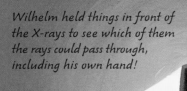

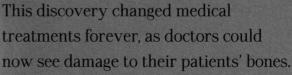

This discovery changed medical treatments forever, as doctors could now see damage to their patients' bones.

Wilhelm didn't patent his work as he believed that his discovery should be available to all. In 1901, he was awarded the Nobel Prize for Physics and donated all of the prize money to Würzburg University, Germany.

MARIE CURIE

Polish physicist and chemist
1867–1934

We now know that radiation is harmful. Marie's notebooks absorbed radiation and are so dangerous that they still can't be touched!

Marie undertook hard physical work to extract elements from pitchblende.

Scientific heroine **Marie Curie** is the only person to have won a Nobel prize in both chemistry and physics. Born Maria Skłodowska in Warsaw, Poland, she developed a love of science by using a chemistry set at home.

Unable to study her passion at a Polish university because women weren't allowed onto scientific courses, Marie studied in secret through an organization called the Flying University. She eventually raised enough money to travel to Paris, and dedicated herself to getting a degree. After university, Marie married a famous scientist, Pierre Curie. They began researching radiation. With Pierre's help, Marie discovered two unknown elements in a rock called pitchblende. They named them polonium and radium.

Not knowing the dangers of radiation, Marie and Pierre felt constantly tired and sick. However, the two were very proud of their discoveries, which would become extremely important for future medical treatments. Pierre carried around a vial of radioactive material to shine in guests' faces at parties, and Marie kept some of it by her bed to provide light after dark.

When Pierre won the Nobel Prize for Physics, he asked that it be awarded to Marie as well. She later won another one for chemistry.

During World War I, Marie invented mobile units to X-ray wounded soldiers. Sadly, she later died from an illness caused by the very radiation she spent her life researching.

Marie and Pierre worked in their back-garden laboratory to make the important discoveries.

GARRETT A. MORGAN

GARRETT A. MORGAN

American inventor and entrepreneur
1877–1963

Garrett Morgan was born bursting with ideas. His parents were former slaves, and he knew he'd have to work harder than most to make his ideas a reality. These ideas would eventually lead him to leave behind an impressive legacy as an accomplished inventor who saved many lives.

Brilliant businessman

Garrett left school at a young age and supported himself by doing odd jobs. Fortunately, he was able to hire a tutor to continue studying. When he was 18, he became a sewing-machine repairman. By the time he was 30, he was the head of his own sewing-machine repair business.

In 1923, Garrett received a patent for his traffic light signal invention. This T-shaped sign indicated to cars in three directions whether they could stop or go.

As his business took off, Garrett became frustrated by repairing other people's things, and wanted to invent products of his own. He was one of the first African-Americans in Cleveland to own a car, and while out driving one day he witnessed an accident involving a pushchair and a car. This inspired him to invent one of the first mechanical traffic lights.

But Garrett didn't stop there. He also created a line of hair-care products and started up a newspaper, the *Cleveland Call*. By now, he had many employees and was becoming a very rich man.

LOCAL INVENTOR SAVES LIVES!

After hearing how firefighters struggled to breathe in scorching, smoke-filled buildings, Garrett came up with his most famous invention: the safety hood. This mask filtered out smoke while allowing the firefighters to breathe cooler air. It was a life-saving device. Unfortunately, Garrett did not receive the recognition he deserved — because he was black, people did not want to accept his ideas. Sometimes, when travelling around to sell the device, he even let a white actor pretend to be the inventor, as some people would not have bought it if they knew the true inventor was African-American.

In recent years, Garrett has gained more appreciation for his impressive ideas and inventions, and the way he tried to improve the world around him.

In 1916, Garrett put his invention to the test. A group of mine workers were trapped under a lake, suffocating in toxic fumes after an explosion. All of the rescuers, including Garrett, wore his safety hood, saving many lives.

THE INCREDIBLE "SAFETY HOOD"

Garrett's breathing hood enabled firefighters to breathe cleaner air in smoky environments. It was taken on by the US Army, and later used as the basis for gas masks during World War I.

Damp cotton wool inside filtered out smoke.

Air reached the mask through two long tubes.

The tubes connected at the back to reach the cleaner, cooler air close to the ground.

MÁRIA TELKES
Hungarian chemist and engineer
1900–1996

Do you have a nickname? Mária Telkes had a great one — the "Sun Queen" — but she didn't get it just because of her sunny nature. Mária's fascination with the Sun began when she was a child, and continued to shine brightly throughout her life. She was a free spirit. At 24, having studied chemistry at Budapest University in Hungary, she planned a brief visit to her uncle in Cleveland, USA. She didn't return for almost 70 years!

In 1925, Mária started work at the Cleveland Clinic — now one of the best hospitals in the USA. There, she made a device to measure electrical currents in the brain. From then on, Mária worked on a series of inventions that would change the world — and lead to her famous nickname.

The solar still

World War II broke out in 1939, and produced a problem that Mária was perfectly suited to solving. Some sailors and airmen found themselves stranded at sea, surrounded by salty seawater that they couldn't drink. Mária invented the solar still, which used the Sun's energy to turn seawater into drinking water.

Seawater enters the still through this funnel.

The contraption produced clean water for the soldiers.

The solar still works by heating up seawater so that it becomes water vapour. As it cools down, it condenses into drinkable water, leaving dirt behind in the mesh.

Queen of green energy

Historically, we have used fossil fuels such as coal to power our world, but these are harmful to the environment and will eventually get used up. Green, or renewable, energy uses resources that won't run out, such as the Sun. Mária designed a solar-powered house, oven, and drinking water device, making her an early pioneer of renewable power. Mária's work was wide-ranging. She advised the

Mária was the first person to create a solar cooker. Carefully angled mirrors caught the Sun's rays to create temperatures of up to 220°C (428°F).

Mária became the first person to receive the Society of Women Engineers Award.

American government on energy, and even worked for NASA developing materials to withstand extreme temperatures in space.

Today, faced with the dangers of climate change, we recognize Mária's important contribution to green energy technology. Renewable energy sources such as the Sun now provide around a quarter of the world's power. However, the potential of solar power was largely untapped before Mária dedicated herself to finding new ways of using it. She was truly visionary.

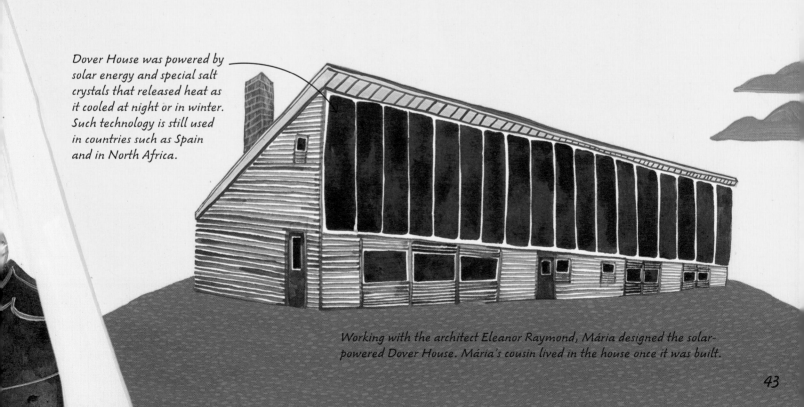

Dover House was powered by solar energy and special salt crystals that released heat as it cooled at night or in winter. Such technology is still used in countries such as Spain and in North Africa.

Working with the architect Eleanor Raymond, Mária designed the solar-powered Dover House. Mária's cousin lived in the house once it was built.

MIN CHUEH CHANG

Chinese biologist • 1908–1991

Min Chueh Chang devoted his life to helping people have babies. Many animals, including humans, have to create eggs and sperm to reproduce, or give birth. Women create egg cells and men make sperm — single cells with a tail that allows them to move. A sperm must fertilize, or join up with, an egg in order to grow into a baby. Some people struggle to have babies naturally, and scientists such as Min developed something called IVF — *in vitro* fertilization. This was a way to join eggs and sperm in a lab, before implanting these fertilized eggs in a woman, ready to grow into babies.

Born in China, Min had a good education. He studied animal psychology, then won an award to go to university abroad — choosing Edinburgh and then Cambridge, UK. It was here that he began his IVF work. He used rabbits to work out the best conditions for joining sperm and eggs.

Min wanted to know whether rabbit sperm and eggs could join outside the body.

Breeding bunnies

Min's key experiment was fertilizing a black rabbit's eggs with a black rabbit's sperm, then transferring the resulting embryo to a white rabbit. The white rabbit gave birth to black baby rabbits — proving beyond doubt that IVF worked. Min remained modest and was very helpful to the scientists who came after him, and who went on to develop IVF treatment for humans.

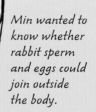

ANNE McLAREN

British scientist • 1927–2007

As a child, **Anne McLaren appeared** in a science-fiction film called *Things to Come*, in which she watched mice being flown to the Moon. It was this, perhaps, that ignited her interest in mice, but she went on to work in a lab rather than star on the big screen!

Anne studied zoology at university, then spent many years experimenting with mice to research how to perform IVF safely. She worked with her husband, Donald Michie, to study how babies grow inside the body. Their three children often joined them in the lab at weekends — would you have liked to have helped Anne with her experiments?

Along with scientist John Biggers, Anne went on to perfect mouse IVF. Their studies included researching how to create healthy eggs, understanding mouse genetics (the unique set of codes, or genes, that make up all living things), and early work on cloning — copying an animal's genes. Together, they paved the way for techniques now used in human IVF.

Anne won many awards during her career. In 1992, she became the Vice-President of the Royal Society — a group of leading scientists dedicated to furthering scientific discovery. She was the first woman in history to hold this position.

Things to Come was the film adaptation of H.G. Wells' popular book, set many years into the future.

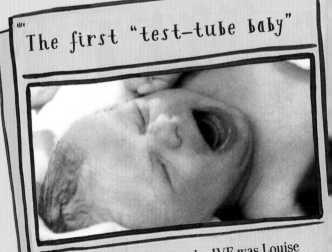

The first "test-tube baby"

The first baby to be born by IVF was Louise Brown, in July 1978 in Oldham, UK. There are now more than 6 million IVF babies in the world.

STEPHANIE KWOLEK

Polish-American chemist
1923–2014

Stephanie originally wanted to be a doctor, but ended up saving lives by creating super strong materials instead. Her parents moved from Poland to the USA, where Stephanie was born. Stephanie's father, Jan, died when she was just 10 years old, but he stimulated her love for science. She went for walks with her dad in the woods, identifying snakes, birds, and flowers. She preserved flowers by pressing them in her record books.

Stephanie's mother, Nellie, was interested in fashion and dressmaking. Stephanie copied her and loved making paper outfits for dolls and stealing time on her mum's sewing machine to make clothes. She thought about becoming a fashion designer, but her mum said that she was too much of a perfectionist — she'd never be happy with her creations! Stephanie would end up working with materials, but not in the world of fashion...

As a child, Stephanie loved designing clothes. Little did she know that she'd go on to create one of the strongest fabrics ever made.

That's when I said, "Aha!" — I knew then and there it was an important discovery.

Bullet-proof vest

Bicycle tyre

Made of strong stuff

At school, Stephanie excelled at science, and read scientific magazines in her spare time. She hoped to become a doctor, but could not afford medical school. Instead, she studied chemistry at university. After graduation, Stephanie worked at a research company called DuPont, which had recently worked on nylon, a new artificial fabric. Next DuPont wanted to create a tough material to reinforce car tyres.

Stephanie, working on her own, produced a liquid that she thought was the answer. She asked a DuPont technician to put her creation through something called a "spinner" to test it, but he refused, thinking it would clog up the machine. However, Stephanie was determined, and very persuasive.

Racing sails

Spacesuit

Army helmet

Kevlar has lots of important uses.

Diving glove

Skis

When her solution went through the spinner, the fibres became five times stronger than steel, and much lighter. This was a material strong enough to protect people from bullets or the freezing temperatures of space. They called it Kevlar.

Stephanie was responsible for 28 inventions during her 40 years at DuPont. However, throughout it all, she remained humble about her work, saying: "At least I hope I'm saving lives. There are very few people in their careers that have the opportunity to do something to benefit mankind."

Kevlar

Kevlar is made of polymers, which are strings of long, chain-like molecules. The polymers in Kevlar line up making it even stronger, more flexible, and able to withstand hot and cold temperatures. These characteristics make Kevlar very desirable for many things, such as tyres, body armour, and even spacesuits.

Stephanie was involved in the development of a material called Nomex, which is used in firefighters' clothing.

Spandex, or Lycra, was another material Stephanie researched. Its flexible properties make it ideal for gym clothing.

DOMINGO SANTO LIOTTA

Argentine doctor • 1924—present

Domingo invented a device that replicated the actions of one of the most complex and essential parts of the human body — the heart. His most vivid childhood memories are of his garden in Diamante, Argentina, where his father, a musician, grew plants such as colourful bougainvillea and sweet-smelling honeysuckle. His older brother, Salvador, went to medical school and Domingo followed in his footsteps, qualifying as a doctor in 1949. For decades, doctors had been developing artificial hearts, but no one had been able to successfully implant one into a human. Domingo set out to crack the problem. He first developed a miniature pump to replace a dog's heart. However, his big breakthrough came when he joined Baylor College in Houston, USA. There, he worked with two other talented doctors, Michael DeBakey and Denton Cooley, to develop a mechanical heart for humans.

Listen to your heart

In 1966, Michael and Domingo implanted a pump to assist the failing heart of a 37-year-old woman, who went on to live for another decade.

Building on this success, Domingo worked with Denton to develop a device that could completely replace a diseased heart. In 1969, Denton implanted the artificial heart into a patient called Haskell Karp, who was dying of heart failure. It kept him alive for three days, as they waited for a donor human heart to arrive — which took an unexpectedly long time! The aeroplane carrying the heart from Boston broke down and had to make an emergency landing. Luckily, a second plane could transport the heart so it could be transplanted into Haskell's chest. Sadly, he died of a lung infection two days later. However, Domingo had succeeded in proving that an artificial heart could keep a human being alive. Since then, there have been several advances in artificial human heart technology.

Denton Cooley (left) implanted the artificial heart designed by Domingo (right).

The Liotta-Cooley Total Artificial Heart that was implanted into Haskell Karp is made from fabric and a stretchy material called silicone.

The heart

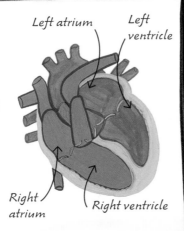

The heart is divided into four chambers. Blood flows into the atria, then the ventricles pump blood to the lungs and body. It beats 705,000 times a week – that's roughly 37 million times over a lifetime!

Left atrium

Left ventricle

Right atrium

Right ventricle

In 2010, the first practical portable artificial heart was implanted. With this device, patients could live comfortably at home while waiting for a heart transplant. However, to this day no machine has been built that can permanently replace the human heart. Something for you to work on, perhaps?

TU YOUYOU

Chinese chemist
1930–present

Tu Youyou has saved the lives of millions around the world. She was born in Ningbo, China, to parents who believed education was most important. However, Youyou's education was disrupted when she fell ill with tuberculosis at 16, missing two years of school. Rather than let this hold her back, the experience spurred her on to become a medicine marvel. She wanted to save others from the suffering she had experienced, so when she went back to school, she started researching medicine. Years later, when tasked with the monumental job of finding a cure for malaria — a deadly disease that claimed 3 million lives a year — Youyou gave it everything she had.

I do not want fame. Every scientist dreams of doing something that can help the world.

Youyou read about ancient Chinese plant remedies and tested them in the lab as part of her malaria research.

Infected mosquitoes spread malaria by biting animals or humans.

Malaria miracle

In the 1970s, malaria was a massive health problem, especially in tropical areas. Youyou was fascinated by ancient Chinese medicine and pored over ancient books to try to find a remedy. The answer came in a book that was more than 1,500 years old. It mentioned a plant — sweet wormwood — as a treatment for fever, and as malaria causes repeated bouts of high fever, this plant seemed relevant. Had a cure finally been found?

Youyou and her team carefully extracted the key ingredient from the plant, called artemisinin. She was so dedicated to her work that she didn't get to spend much time with her children. She even volunteered to try the medicine on herself first! When she knew the drug was safe, she used it on patients and cured 21 people. They had invented a brand new life-saving drug!

Still, it was more than 20 years before Youyou's breakthrough was known around the world. Today, she is recognized as one of the leading pioneers in malarial treatment, winning the Nobel Prize in Medicine in 2015.

If a person takes anti-malaria drugs soon after catching the disease, it's almost certain they will make a full recovery.

Beating malaria

Deaths from malaria have dropped dramatically since the drugs Youyou helped develop have been widely available.

Deaths from malaria per year

800,000
600,000
400,000
200,000
0

2000   2005   2010   2015

Year

The sweet wormwood plant, native to Asia, contains a malaria-fighting ingredient.

PATRICIA BATH

Patricia knew from a young age that she wanted to be a doctor. Playing pretend games with her friends, she always insisted on being the one holding the stethoscope. Growing up in Harlem, New York City, Patricia didn't have a lot of money but she did very well at school, particularly in biology, and won several awards for scientific research. Patricia's father, Rupert, had travelled widely in the navy and inspired her to think about the world beyond their city. Her mother, Gladys, bought Patricia a chemistry set and worked as a cleaner to save enough money to send Patricia to medical school. After qualifying as a doctor, Patricia became the first African-American to complete a residency, or placement, in ophthalmology (eye medicine) at New York University. Working at Harlem Hospital during her studies, Patricia had noticed that African-Americans were twice as likely to suffer from blindness than her other patients because they had never seen an eye doctor. She organized community care, which provided eye tests to people without access to them. Regular testing meant that people could get prompt treatment to prevent blindness, and children with poor eyesight could be given glasses so they would do better at school.

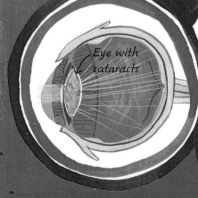

Eye with cataracts

Healthy eye

In healthy eyes, light hits the back of the eye in one spot, creating a clear image. Eyes with cataracts have cloudy lenses, which distorts vision. If left untreated, cataracts can cause blindness.

Patricia's invention points a laser at the lens of the eye. The lens is melted and replaced with an artificial one, saving the person's sight.

The laser is fired 1 mm (0.03 in) into the eye.

The cataract is vaporized.

The gift of sight

In 1981, Patricia had an idea for a device that could help save the sight of people who had developed cataracts, a disease that makes your vision go misty. It was a very advanced idea for the time. However, Patricia was not taken seriously and as a black woman, people weren't willing to fund her invention in the USA. But she refused to give up. She travelled to Europe and worked at various medical institutes as she developed her invention. It took years to create, but in 1988 she succeeded, becoming the first African-American female doctor to receive a medical patent. For the rest of her life, Patricia travelled extensively, helping to improve eye surgery across the world. However, her proudest moment was restoring the sight of a woman in North Africa who had been blind for 30 years.

"The ability to restore sight is the ultimate reward."

RACHEL ZIMMERMAN
Canadian space scientist
1972–present

The Perseid meteor shower peaks in mid-August each year.

Despite being deaf and blind, Helen Keller achieved success as a writer and lecturer.

Louis Braille's system of writing has helped millions of blind people read.

A s a child, **Rachel Zimmerman wanted to be an astronaut.** When she grew up, she became the next best thing — a space scientist. She now encourages thousands of students to reach for the stars. Born in Ontario, Canada, Rachel was motivated by her parents to think about science from an early age. Even before she started going to school, she performed experiments in the bath. One cold night, her parents took Rachel and her brother out into a field to gaze at the Perseid meteor shower crossing the dark sky — watching it from under a warm blanket was better than any firework display!

Always highly inquisitive, Rachel loved reading and was especially enthusiastic about astronomy. She was also fascinated by Louis Braille, who invented a writing system of raised dots for blind people to read by touch — and Helen Keller, who famously learned to communicate, despite being deaf and blind.

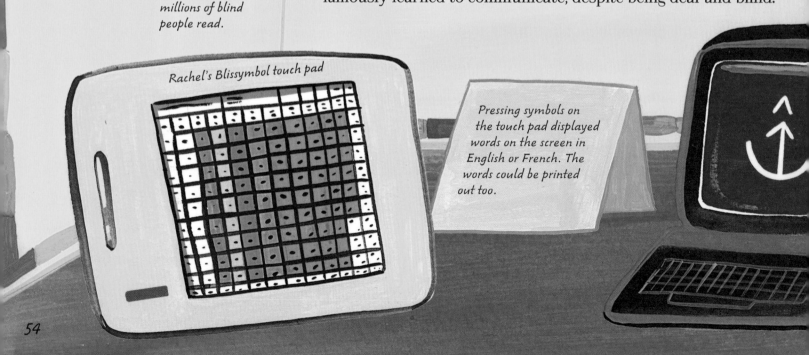

Rachel's Blissymbol touch pad

Pressing symbols on the touch pad displayed words on the screen in English or French. The words could be printed out too.

54

Speaking through symbols

At the age of 12, Rachel wrote a computer program that could help people with severe disabilities to communicate using pictures known as Blissymbols. It was a school project at first, but it soon developed into the Blissymbol printer — a device that lets people with a brain disorder called cerebral palsy, who often struggle to communicate, use a simple touch pad to express their ideas and feelings. Her invention won a silver medal at the Canada-Wide Science Fair in 1985.

After gaining degrees in physics and space studies, Rachel joined NASA. She has led many educational projects for students at its Jet Propulsion Laboratory in California. Her work has also used space technology to make life easier for people with disabilities.

Rachel was also involved in the Cassini mission, which sent a probe to Saturn and its moons. And she's still hoping to become an astronaut one day...

Charles K. Bliss invented a language of symbols, called Blissymbols, in the 1940s.

Mind   Give   Knowledge

House   Wheel   Sun

Congratulations

I was born a scientist, asking questions about the world around me, experimenting, seeking answers.

VEENA SAHAJWALLA

Indian–Australian engineer and professor

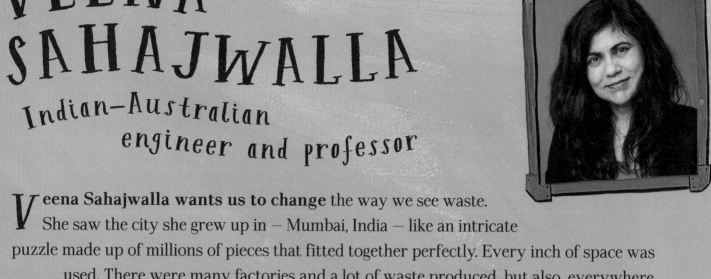

Veena Sahajwalla wants us to change the way we see waste. She saw the city she grew up in — Mumbai, India — like an intricate puzzle made up of millions of pieces that fitted together perfectly. Every inch of space was used. There were many factories and a lot of waste produced, but also, everywhere Veena turned, she saw people repurposing, fixing, and selling things that had been thrown away by others. She felt inspired.

As a child, Veena liked taking objects apart to find out how they worked — even if it meant breaking things in the process. Once, when testing how tough a coconut shell was, she accidentally smashed a ceramic sink! This curiosity about materials and tendency to take risks stayed with Veena into adulthood, and ultimately led to her biggest scientific breakthrough.

Used tyres and plastics were injected into furnaces that burned at 1,500°C (2,732°F) to create the chemical reactions that make steel.

Nerves of steel

After university, Veena moved to Australia to work as a scientist. She became interested in metals, and wondered whether there was a way to reuse waste to make steel. She experimented with old rubber tyres and found that when they were melted down, they had parts that were useful in creating steel. She had no idea what would happen when these tyre particles were added to the steel-making furnace — it might have worked, but it could have blown up! Luckily, the risk paid off — "Waste warrior" Veena had invented "Green Steel" technology. The metal produced was just as strong as normal steel and proved Veena's view that we should value waste. She doesn't see any waste as worthless — all materials have the potential to be useful.

The "Green Steel" process has prevented more than 2 million tyres from ending up in rubbish dumps.

Another exciting eco project Veena has been involved in is creating micro factories. Unlike traditional factories, micro factories are small and mobile, so they can be brought directly to the waste. This makes small-scale recycling much easier. When Veena first started re-purposing materials, she found that there wasn't much support and people were sceptical. In recent years, however, the public have become much more serious about recycling. Many people despair about how much waste fills our world, but Veena remains hopeful for the future.

Veena has created tiles made from recycled materials such as glass.

YUSUF MUHAMMAD

British engineer and designer
1983–present

Yusuf transformed an early love of art into a love of inventing. He's determined to use his ideas and talent as an engineer to help people and improve the world.

As a boy, Yusuf could often be found sketching in his notebooks. When he was 18, he decided to go to university. You can't study inventing, but Yusuf chose subjects as close to it as possible, such as Materials and Design. He soon came up with the idea for his first co-invention along with some other students. They wanted to invent something that could improve how fires were put out.

The group spoke to a firefighter, who told them he used a hose to spray a mist of water into a burning room before entering. The mist reduced the high temperature — making it safer for a firefighter to enter — and stopped the fire from growing. Yusuf imagined a device that would make a cloud-like spray of water if it detected a fire. He and his group worked on their idea and won a £25,000 prize to build the invention, which they named "Automist". It uses 90 per cent less water than hoses or sprinklers. One of Yusuf's proudest moments came when he learned that the Automist had saved a life.

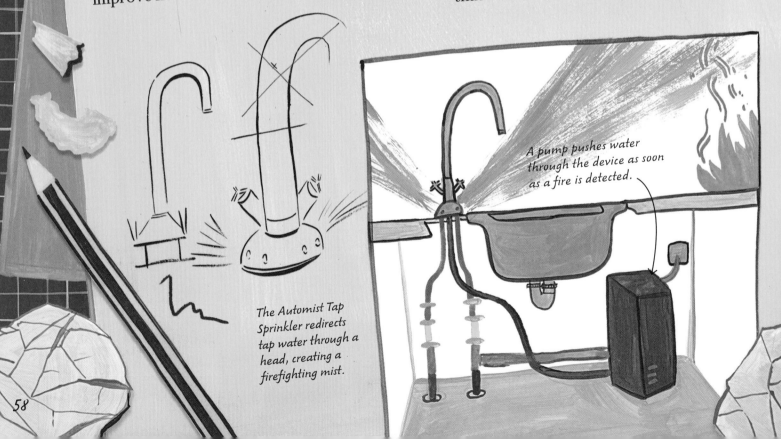

The Automist Tap Sprinkler redirects tap water through a head, creating a firefighting mist.

A pump pushes water through the device as soon as a fire is detected.

Yusuf believes that failure is important — you never get it right the first time.

Inventions with a conscience

Yusuf has designed many more inventions since the Automist, with a focus on helping people. These include creating a special snowboard for a man who was keen to get back to the mountains after a brain injury, and an artificial foot that allowed a girl to ballet dance.

Yusuf learned through inventing that failure is an important part of achieving success. Failures showed him what was wrong with his inventions, so that he could improve them until they worked perfectly. The most important thing, he says, is not to give up.

Yusuf's snowboard allows its user to lean on built-in crutches. The crutches also help the snowboarder to steer.

Yusuf creates life-changing inventions for individuals.

Yusuf heard about a 12-year-old girl who had dreams of becoming a ballerina, but struggled to get into certain positions because of her prosthetic leg. He designed an artificial foot to help her.

Yusuf's artificial foot allowed the girl to perform a demi-pointe position (balancing on the toes).

WILLIAM KAMKWAMBA

Malawian innovator and author
1987–present

William built a series of windmills and solar panels to power the lights in his family home.

When he invented a power-generating windmill from scrap, William didn't realize that he would end up inspiring people around the world. He grew up in a corn-farming family near Kasungu, a remote part of Malawi, Africa. In 2002, a terrible famine struck the country, and Kasungu was among the worst hit areas. During the famine, William and his family ate just three mouthfuls of ground-up corn a day. Aged 14, William was forced to drop out of school because his family couldn't afford the fees. Instead, he studied by himself at the library, and developed an interest in physics. One day, he came across a science textbook that explained how windmills could produce electricity. William wondered whether he could build a windmill himself to generate electricity for the whole village.

The make-do windmill

William scavenged materials from a scrapyard and used parts of an old bicycle. With these, he built a windmill propped up on three tall wooden sticks that he connected with wire to his house. He generated enough electricity to power the lights in his family's home, as well as two radios. Later, he built a bigger windmill that could pump water into the fields to help crops grow. Word spread about William's windmills, and soon queues of people formed around his house, taking turns to charge their phones.

Since then, William's life has changed dramatically. He was able to go back to school, and went on to university to study engineering. He continues to help his local community and beyond, building handy devices such as a water well with a solar-powered pump.

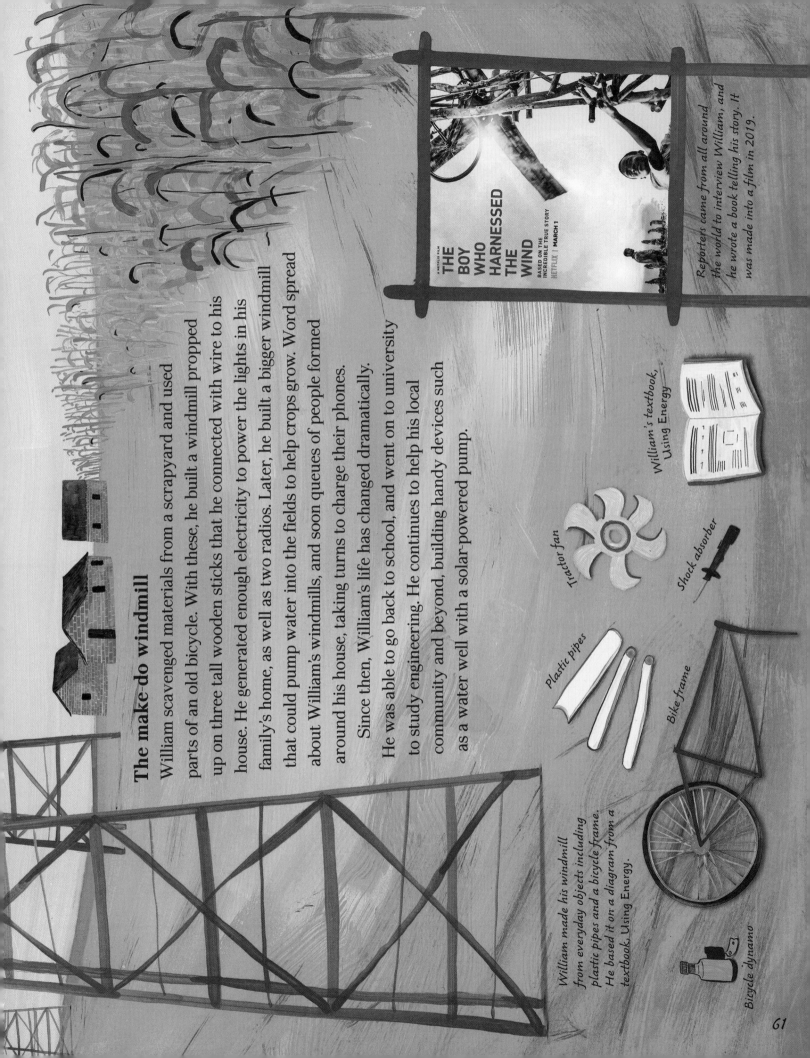

THE
BOY
WHO
HARNESSED
THE
WIND

A NETFLIX FILM

BASED ON THE
INCREDIBLE TRUE STORY

NETFLIX | MARCH 1

Reporters came from all around the world to interview William, and he wrote a book telling his story. It was made into a film in 2019.

William's textbook, Using Energy

Tractor fan

Shock absorber

Plastic pipes

Bike frame

William made his windmill from everyday objects including plastic pipes and a bicycle frame. He based it on a diagram from a textbook, Using Energy.

Bicycle dynamo

RUTH AMOS
Engineer and YouTuber
1989–present

Ruth Amos has been inventing since she was at school. When Ruth was 16, a teacher challenged her to design something that would help his father move around the house after he suffered a stroke. She came up with the StairSteady. This simple device slides and locks onto stair banisters and allows people to stabilize themselves with both hands as they climb or descend. Ruth's inexpensive invention has helped differently abled people of all ages, and won her a national engineering award.

Ruth's childhood was filled with activities that allowed her imagination to flourish — she loved creating assault courses in the garden, building models, and hosting her own pretend radio show. Ruth's dad, a computer expert, taught her programming and modified computer games to give her unlimited lives. Her grandparents, too, would help her to write scripts and make costumes for performances she put on with her siblings. After leaving school, Ruth decided to put her active imagination to use and created the YouTube channel *Kids Invent Stuff* with the engineer Shawn Brown. Children send in ideas for inventions, and Ruth and Shawn build them on camera — however weird and wacky the concepts might sound!

Imagination running wild

On their YouTube channel, Ruth and Shawn encourage kids to find solutions to everyday problems. For instance, one competition involved thinking up ideas to improve city streets. Children submitted lots of interesting ideas, such as a bin that blows bubbles after you use it. In the end, they built a suit that sucks up litter.

Ruth aims to get children excited about engineering through awe-inspiring projects, such as a piano that shoots fire when played!

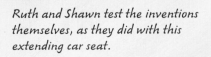

Ruth and Shawn test the inventions themselves, as they did with this extending car seat.

Ruth noticed that many of the children she worked with, particularly the girls, lacked confidence in their ability. She started a campaign called "Girls With Drills" with the engineer Kisha Bradley, to encourage young female inventors from all backgrounds. In all of her work, Ruth's aim is to inspire young people to learn about engineering and to think creatively.

Some of the inventions are brilliantly silly, such as this unicorn that poops sweets!

Kids Invent Stuff

Ruth and Shawn have brought dozens of wonderfully bizarre inventions to life, from a sneeze-activated flamethrower, to a robotic shopping trolley.

DEEPIKA KURUP

American scientist
1998–present

Many of us take clean drinking water for granted but, aged 14, Deepika Kurup found that this was not the case for everyone around the world.

While visiting her family in India, Deepika was told to drink only bottled or boiled water. However, she was shocked to see people queueing in long lines in the street to fill buckets with dirty water from a tap. The sight of children her age being, in her own words, "forced to drink water that I felt was too dirty to touch", made her realize just how serious the world's clean water problem was.

After Deepika returned home to New Hampshire, USA, she went online and did some research. She discovered that more than 600 million people around the world are without access to a clean water source, and felt compelled to do something to help. Deepika asked her parents if she could be home-schooled so that she'd have more time to study and develop ways to purify water.

Deepika set up a makeshift laboratory in her parents' garage.

"Water is a universal human right."

The power of the Sun

In her research, Deepika learned about solar purification, which uses rays from the Sun to kill harmful bacteria — tiny living creatures — in water. However, she found that existing methods were expensive and potentially dangerous.

After her parents kicked Deepika out of the kitchen laboratory she'd set up, she moved her work into the garage. Through a long process of trial and error, she eventually invented a cheap and eco-friendly method to clean water using solar power. In 2012, Deepika entered a national science competition with an early model of her invention and won, receiving the title "America's Top Young Scientist".

Deepika went on to study to become a doctor and hopes to improve the health of people around the world. She continues to campaign for clean water, saying: "Just as water drops come together to form oceans, I believe that we all must come together when tackling this global problem."

Deepika carried out many experiments to make sure her water purification system worked.

Unclean water is stored in the tank.

Water flows through the pipes and is purified using solar power.

Clean, drinkable water comes out of the other end.

65

RICHARD TURERE

Maasai inventor • 2000–present

Richard is one of the youngest inventors in this book and also one of the bravest — he scares lions! Richard is a Maasai, a member of an African tribe whose way of life revolves around keeping cattle. When Maasai boys are young, usually around nine, they are given an important job — they have to go out into the countryside and look after the cattle on which their families depend. However, where Richard lives, on the edge of the Nairobi National Park, in Kenya, there are many dangerous animals, such as leopards, hyenas, and lions, that threaten the cattle. When it was Richard's turn to protect the cattle, his herd was being badly affected by lion attacks. He was worried that other members of the tribe might respond by killing the lions — something he didn't want to happen. Richard was determined to come up with a peaceful solution that would keep his cows, and his family, safe.

Richard has travelled the world to tell the tale of how he came up with his life-saving invention at such a young age.

Solar panel

Light bulb

Switch

Battery

Lion Lights are now widely used across Kenya, because of how simple and cheap they are to set up.

LION LIGHTS
100% effective

BUILD: 2012
BY
TURE RE Jnr

Richard's original Lion Lights sign, which he built when he was 12 years old.

Trick of the light

Richard tried using scarecrows to frighten the predators, but this didn't work — lions aren't stupid. Then, one night, when he was bravely walking outside with a torch, he found that the lions stayed away from the light. So Richard experimented with ways to make lights appear to move, without having to endanger himself by patrolling at night. First he took his mum's radio apart — hopefully she wasn't too cross — and taught himself about electronics. Then he got hold of an old car battery and a solar panel and connected them to a string of torches that flashed on and off along a fence. It worked! The lions were tricked into thinking that someone was there.

Ever since then, his family have had no more cattle eaten by lions, and as a result no lions have been killed either. The Lion Lights were such a success that other Maasai groups adopted this effective way of dealing with predators. The invention led Richard to gain a scholarship into one of Kenya's best schools. He remains fascinated by technology and plans to learn enough to become a pilot one day.

Maasai community

The Maasai are a group of people, or tribe, that live in Kenya and northern Tanzania, Africa. They live off the land and have kept many of their old traditions. Maasai live in huts in family compounds arranged in a circle, known as *manyattas*.

HELPING AT HOME

Look around your home. From your television to your toys, almost every item that surrounds you was once an idea dreamed up by an inventor. Whether they help us with household tasks or are just for entertainment, these are the inventions many of us use every day.

JOHN HARINGTON

British courtier and writer
1560–1612

We sit on the toilet every day, but have you ever thought about how this invention came to be? John Harington, who once wrote a rambling book about poo, invented the first flushing lavatory. He was a courtier of Queen Elizabeth I, entertaining her with rude stories that your parents wouldn't like — so we won't repeat them. His jokes got so bad that, in 1584, the Queen banned him from the court. His punishment was that he couldn't return until he had translated a very long poem. However, much to everybody's surprise, John managed to complete his homework.

Queen Elizabeth banished John, making him translate the Italian poem Orlando Furioso.

When the handle on the seat was turned, water swept the toilet's contents away.

John did something else during his exile — he built the first-ever lavatory. He named his loo the "Ajax" ("jakes" was a slang word for toilet). It had a huge wooden seat, a water tank, and a pipe taking sewage away, which reduced bad smells. The queen eventually forgave John for his naughty jokes, and in 1591 visited his house. John proudly showed her his invention and, while we don't know whether she tried it out herself, she was so impressed that she asked him to install one for her too. John, ever the fan of toilet humour, called his toilet the "throne".

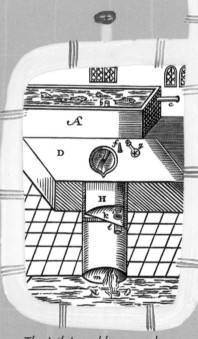

The toilet used levers and weights to pour water from a cistern and to open a valve that let waste flow away.

THOMAS CRAPPER

British plumber
1836–1910

Many myths surround **Thomas Crapper's life**, including that he invented the toilet, that he was knighted, and even that he didn't actually exist. However, these rumours are all made up, so let's find out the truth...

Thomas was a plumber from Yorkshire, UK, who learned the trade from his elder brother. He started a business building toilets and was the first person to create a bathroom showroom in his shop. Thomas made many improvements to the toilet — for instance, inventing the S-bend pipe fitting, which traps smells.

Thomas sold baths in his shop, named Thomas Crapper & Co, in London, UK.

These plumbing pioneers brought toilets from the private realm to the wider public.

Thomas Crapper products were known for their exceptional quality, and Edward, Prince of Wales bought 30 of their finest loos.

John and Thomas' work was of huge importance. Before flushing toilets were widely used, water-borne diseases killed many thousands of people. The flushing toilet was key to changing this in many countries, but sadly there are still places in the world where people die due to a lack of proper plumbing.

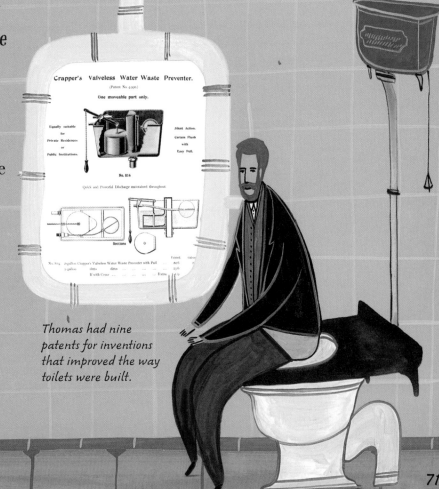

Thomas had nine patents for inventions that improved the way toilets were built.

BARTOLOMEO CRISTOFORI

Italian instrument maker
1655–1731

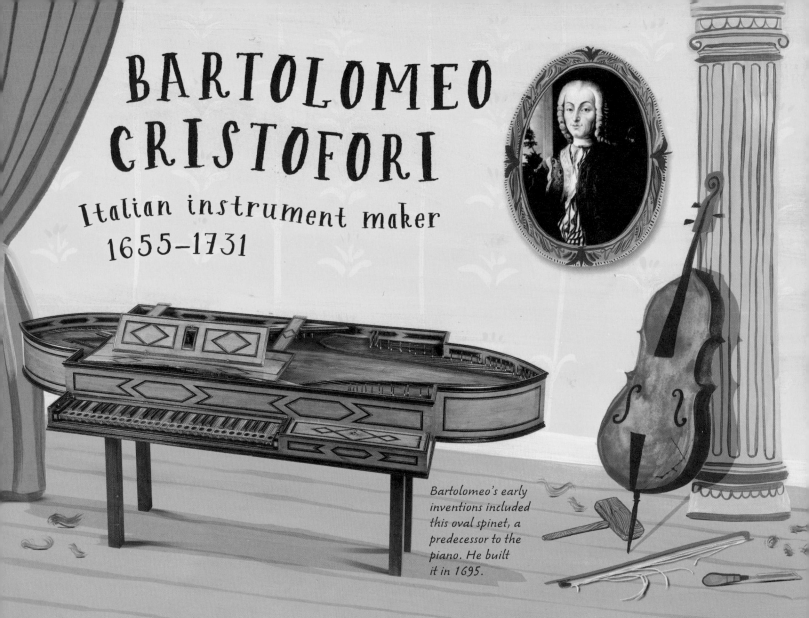

Bartolomeo's early inventions included this oval spinet, a predecessor to the piano. He built it in 1695.

The invention of the piano changed the way we play music forever, and it's all thanks to one man — Bartolomeo Cristofori. Although little is known about Bartolomeo's life, he definitely left his mark on the world when he built his first piano during the first decade of the 18th century. Bartolomeo kept detailed written records of his instruments, and some of his pianos still exist today.

Born in Padua, Italy, Bartolomeo began working for Prince Ferdinand de Medici in 1688. The Medici family ruled parts of modern-day Italy, and were very wealthy. They owned many fine instruments, and Bartolomeo was extremely skilled at taking care of them. He mostly maintained and repaired the prince's extensive collection of wooden harpsichords (a type of musical instrument that is similar to a piano, but its strings are plucked instead of hammered when played). Working with such beautifully crafted instruments, Bartolomeo was inspired to create an instrument of his own.

Bartolomeo's invention was revolutionary in the musical world. The keys on his pianos respond to pressure — the harder you press, the louder the resulting musical note. This meant that a musician could now play with more expression than a harpsichord. Bartolomeo's pianos became much more popular than harpsichords as they had a wider range of sound.

Fragile! Do not touch!

Bartolomeo's instruments were superbly well made and of the highest quality. Only three of his pianos are still in existence: one in New York, USA, one in Leipzig, Germany, and the final piano is in Bartolomeo's hometown in Italy. These pianos are now so delicate and fragile that the wood from which they are made could split if touched. Nobody is allowed to play them in case they fall apart!

Bartolomeo's contributions to the world of music were massive — more people learn to play the piano than any other instrument. Next time you listen to a song, see whether you can hear a piano being played!

Ferdinand de Medici funded Bartolomeo's musical inventions.

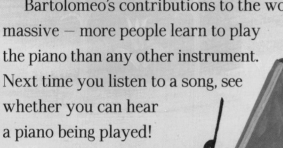

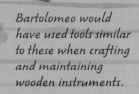
Bartolomeo would have used tools similar to these when crafting and maintaining wooden instruments.

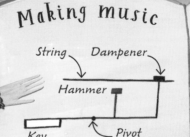

Making music

String   Dampener
Hammer
Key   Pivot

When a piano key is not being pressed, the hammer doesn't touch the string.

When a key is being pressed, the hammer hits the string and makes a sound.

Piano man

Bartolomeo's pianofortes — or pianos for short — were delicately crafted. Modern-day pianos work in the same way as Bartolomeo's.

WALTER HUNT

American inventor
1796–1859

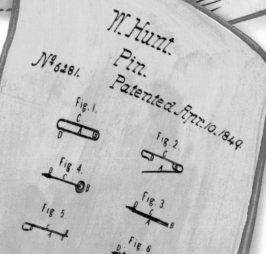

Very few inventions have been used by nearly everybody, but Walter Hunt's is one exception. He made the first safety pin simply by bending a piece of springy wire. It took him just three hours, and he sold the design for only $400, but the company that bought it made millions!

Walter was forever thinking of how to solve problems with ingenious new machines and tools. His first known invention came when he improved a machine that spun a crop called flax into thread at a cloth mill. He then moved to New York City and patented around 100 inventions, including an ice-breaker, a fountain pen, an inkwell, a repeating rifle, a machine for making nails, a tree saw, and a knife sharpener! Walter never made much money, but that didn't stop him. His ambition was to do good and fiddle with things to make them better.

Walter produced a wide range of inventions. Many have become well-known household objects.

Walter's safety pin patent

The safety pin

Walter created the pin's safety catch by coiling a length of wire into a spring that clasped into the case. He thought this secure fastening would be perfect on clothes or babies' nappies, as it would protect people from accidentally pricking themselves.

Walter invented purely for the joy of it.

Walking on the ceiling

Have you ever wished you could walk along walls or upside down on the ceiling? Walter designed suction cup shoes so that circus performers could do just that, although we don't know how well they worked — hopefully nobody fell from the ceiling! More famous and useful was the sewing machine he invented. The story goes that he didn't sell this design because he was worried that women who earned money as seamstresses — sewing and repairing clothes — might be put out of work. Eventually, another inventor made lots of money with a patent for something similar. Walter might not have been rich, but he will go down in history as one of the world's most creative and kind-hearted inventors.

Inside Walter's sewing machine

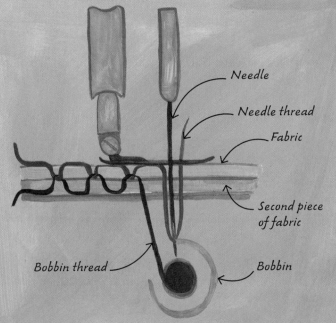

- Needle
- Needle thread
- Fabric
- Second piece of fabric
- Bobbin thread
- Bobbin

Modern sewing machines still use the mechanism invented by Walter Hunt. They stitch fabric together much more quickly than doing it by hand.

The word "lumière" means "light" in French — a fitting name for the Lumière brothers, who were behind the birth of cinema.

As boys, Auguste and Louis were brilliant at science. When their father's photography business was failing, they put their scientific skill to good use by developing an ingenious new way to process film, known as the "dry plate" method. This boosted business enough for the company to avoid bankruptcy.

The brothers' dad helped them out too. He told them about Thomas Edison's kinetoscope, which allowed a single person to view moving pictures through a peephole. Auguste and Louis began to wonder whether they could develop something similar that would allow many people to view the images at the same time...

The Cinématographe

This device was able to record moving images as well as play them back for an audience through its built-in projector.

THE LUMIÈRE BROTHERS
French film-makers

Auguste • 1862–1954
Louis • 1864–1948

The first film screening

The Lumière brothers heard that an American named George Eastman had invented a way to take photographs on flexible rolls of film. Inspired, they used a long strip of film to take many photos in a row, and projected them onto a screen using light. If they could drive the film forward, showing the photos one after the other, it would look as though the images were moving. However, they had trouble thinking of a way to propel the film. Eventually, inspiration struck Louis while in bed ill, in the form of his mother's sewing machine. He saw how it used a wheel to move the needle, and thought they could adapt this idea. By 1895, they had patented a design.

The first film the brothers recorded was of workers leaving their dad's factory, which they screened to a small audience in a Parisian café. Auguste and Louis went on to make more films and travelled the world showing their short clips. These films are important records of how people lived more than 100 years ago.

Posters advertising the Lumière brothers' films depict the excitement of audiences when viewing moving pictures for the first time.

Audiences were terrified when they first watched the film The Arrival of a Train at La Ciotat. *They ducked under their seats thinking that the train was real!*

ALEXANDER GRAHAM BELL
Scottish scientist and engineer
1847–1922

A **theme of communication ran through** Alexander Bell's life. His mother, Eliza, became deaf when he was 12 years old, and the woman he later married, Mabel, was also deaf. Alexander's dad was an expert in elocution — ensuring words are spoken correctly — and created the Visible Alphabet to help deaf people learn to talk. Together, these influences led Alexander to an invention that would change the way we communicate forever.

Aleck, as his family knew him, was a playful boy who loved experimenting. His early experiments involved convincing people that his family dog, Trouve, could talk. First, he taught the dog to growl continuously, then he mischievously moved the dog's lips, tricking his audience into thinking the dog was speaking because the noises sounded like human words.

Aleck used treats to train Trouve, the family dog, to "talk".

Alexander spoke into the transmitter.

78

Joining the family business

The Bells decided to emigrate to Canada after the tragic deaths of both of Aleck's brothers. It was there that Aleck began teaching in deaf schools using his dad's Visible Alphabet system. He then moved to the USA, opening a successful training school for teachers of the deaf in Boston, and later becoming a professor at Boston University.

Mr Watson, come here, I want to see you.

These are the first words that Thomas Watson heard through the receiver.

Students at Alexander's school, founded in 1872.

Alexander opened the long-distance line between New York and Chicago in 1892.

The telephone

Alexander's invention was made up of two main parts. The transmitter transformed sounds into electrical signals that could travel along a wire. At the other end, the receiver converted the signals back into sounds.

Aleck was interested in communications technology and hired Thomas Watson as his assistant. Together, they experimented with ways of transmitting sound along wires. The very first phone call is said to have been an accident. While they were experimenting, Alexander spilled some battery acid. He called for Thomas to help him and Thomas heard this through the receiver. In 1876, they made the world's first telephone and within a year the Bell Telephone Company was created. Aleck quickly became world-famous, and a very rich man! Later, he demonstrated his phone to Queen Victoria, who called it "most extraordinary".

Aleck continued other inventing pursuits, including a metal detector and a powered aircraft, until his death in 1922. The American telephone lines went silent for one minute in his honour.

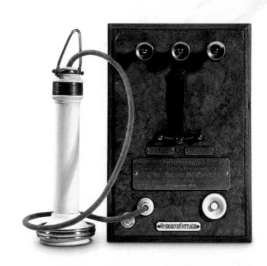

Alexander received a patent for his telephone in 1876.

THOMAS EDISON

American inventor and entrepreneur 1847–1931

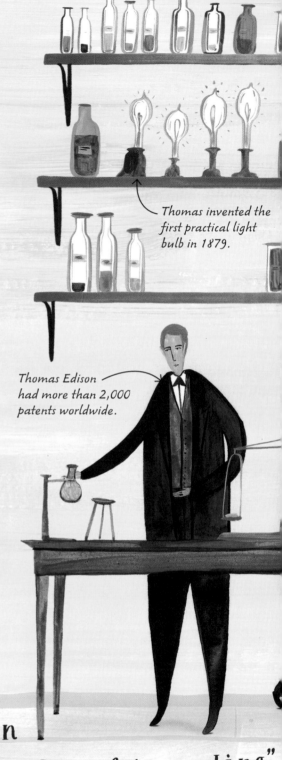

Thomas invented the first practical light bulb in 1879.

Thomas Edison had more than 2,000 patents worldwide.

Thomas Edison is one of the most famous inventors of all time. Growing up, he had a hard time concentrating at school, so his mother decided to teach him at home instead, and Thomas did science experiments in the basement. Even as a child, Thomas was a smart businessman. He sold snacks on the railway and printed his own newspaper, the *Grand Trunk Herald*. He even set up a small laboratory in the baggage car of a train. However, after accidentally starting a fire, Thomas was kicked off the train and had to sell newspapers at the stations. When he was 15, something happened that changed his life. Thomas saved a child from being struck by a train, and to thank him, the child's father taught Thomas how to use a telegraph — a way of sending messages along wires.

Thomas was known as the "inventor of inventing".

Phonograph

In 1877, Thomas invented the phonograph. It was the first machine capable of recording and playing back sounds. Recordings were imprinted on tinfoil-covered cylinders and only lasted a few seconds. The first words he spoke into the phonograph were, "Mary had a little lamb".

The mouthpiece

To work the phonograph you rotated the handle.

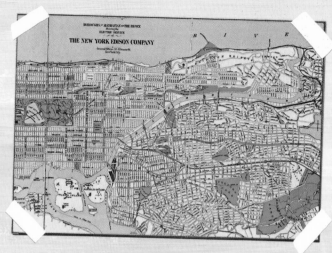

Thomas installed his electric light bulbs inside buildings, and built power plants to generate electricity. Then he built an electric grid that distributed electricity over the city of New York, shown here.

William Kennedy Dickson, who worked for Thomas, developed the kinetoscope.

Electric dreams

During the next six years, Thomas worked as a telegraph operator passing messages around the USA. From 1866, he worked the night shift at a company in Louisville, Kentucky. He liked working at night because he could work on his experiments, until he was fired one day for spilling acid on his boss' desk. During this period, Thomas became very interested in electricity, and his first patent was for a machine that electronically recorded votes. In 1874, he invented a telegraph that could send four messages simultaneously.

Kinetoscope

This was the first movie viewer. Spectators peeped through a hole to watch films that were only 15 seconds long. In 1893, Thomas built the first American film studio and recorded popular circus performers.

In 1876, Thomas established a huge laboratory at Menlo Park, and employed scientists to research and develop new inventions. It was here that Thomas' most famous inventions were born, including the phonograph, the electric light bulb, and the kinetoscope. People were so astounded by his inventions that Thomas was given the nickname, "The Wizard of Menlo Park".

SARAH ELISABETH GOODE

American entrepreneur
c.1850–1905

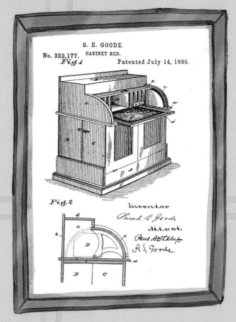

The versatile cabinet bed was designed complete with usable drawers and storage space.

Sarah's cabinet bed could fold up to be used as a desk or side table.

S arah Jacobs was born into slavery. Yet despite the lack of respect she faced as a formerly enslaved black woman, she became one of the first African-American women to receive a patent — an amazing achievement.

Growing up as an enslaved person, it is unlikely that Sarah received much of an education. When slavery was eventually banned, enslaved people, like Sarah, were able to claim their freedom. However, life was still very tough. Discrimination was widespread, and most people who had been enslaved were very poor.

The slave trade

For hundreds of years, Europeans shipped many millions of African people to the USA where they were forced to work as slaves. Enslaved people had their rights taken away and were treated like property. Slavery was eventually banned in the USA in 1865.

The future of furniture

Sarah's space-saving solution inspired future furniture. The Murphy bed, which can be folded flat against a wall, was patented in 1900. These days, multi-functional furniture is common in homes around the world, such as stairs that double up as drawers.

The folding Murphy bed, which came after Sarah's invention, is now used by many people who live in small homes.

A big invention in a small space

Once she was freed, Sarah, still a teenager, moved to Chicago, where she met and married a carpenter named Archibald Goode. Together, they opened a furniture store. Their customers were mostly families who lived in very cramped apartments, in such crowded conditions that there was hardly any room for furniture. Sarah was determined to help solve this problem. She designed a bed which could be folded away into a writing desk during the day. Archibald used his carpentry skills to build it, and Sarah named it the "cabinet bed".

Sarah must have been extremely proud to be one of the first black women to own a patent, when she was granted one in July 1885. Given all of the difficulties she encountered in life, Sarah is rightly remembered as a courageous and ingenious inventor.

KITCHEN CREATIONS

Until the end of the 19th century, people had to light a fire to cook food. As electricity became more widespread and well-off households were less reliant on servants, more and more handy home appliances began to be invented. These devices reduced the time that people, typically women, spent in the kitchen, freeing them up to do other things, such as go to work.

Automatic dishwasher

Josephine Cochrane was annoyed by clumsy servants chipping her best china plates. She didn't want to get her hands wet herself, so she designed an automatic dishwasher. She received a patent for her product in 1886.

Canned food

Canning keeps food fresh by sealing it. Frenchman Nicolas Appert invented canned food in 1809, after the military leader Napoleon offered a prize to anyone who could find a way of preserving food for his armies.

Radio

Radio was invented by the Italian Guglielmo Marconi, who never went to school. He sent his first radio signal in 1895. However, he wouldn't have listened to it in the kitchen, as radio programmes weren't broadcast for another 20 years or so.

Microwave oven

When Percy Spencer was studying radar (a navigational aid) he found that it had melted a chocolate bar in his pocket. He'd discovered a new, fast way of heating up food and filed a patent for it in 1945.

Non-stick frying pan

Non-stick frying pans came after the discovery of Teflon by the chemist Roy Plunkett, in 1938. A coating of Teflon on a pan stops things sticking to it by reducing resistance, but it still doesn't stop bad cooks from burning food!

Toaster

Charles Strite hated burning his toast at breakfast, so in 1919 he invented a toaster that would automatically pop up. Previous toasters weren't very safe, and only toasted one side of bread at a time — Charles' machine heated both sides of the slice.

CLARENCE BIRDSEYE

American entrepreneur and naturalist • 1886–1956

Inuit people

Inuit is a name for the group of peoples who live in the cold Arctic regions of North America and Greenland. They have invented many ways to hunt food and survive in this harsh landscape.

Clarence was never called by his proper name, but instead "Bob" or, more frequently, "Bugs". He was given this nickname by his school friends who teased him for his interest in insects and animals. When he was older, Clarence joined the United States Agriculture Department as an assistant naturalist, and was sent on missions all over the country to study the local wildlife. On one expedition to the American West, he caught hundreds of small mammals with little bugs or ticks in their fur. Thanks to Clarence's work, these ticks were found to cause a dangerous illness called Rocky Mountain spotted fever.

From 1912 to 1915, Clarence lived in Labrador, Canada, where temperatures can fall below -40°C (-40°F). He watched the local Inuit people fish under the ice. Clarence learned that the fish they caught, which froze rapidly in the open air, tasted nicer than frozen fish bought in shops. At the time, the usual way of freezing food was to cool it slowly in a refrigerator, which caused ice crystals to form on the food, making it mushy when reheated. Inspired by the Inuit people, Clarence founded a company that produced frozen food using a quick-freezing method.

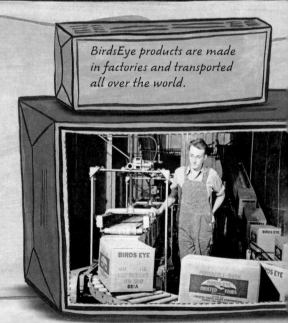

BirdsEye products are made in factories and transported all over the world.

An early advert called BirdsEye frozen peas "as gloriously green as any you will see next summer".

Inuit ice fishing involves lowering bait into a hole in the ice. This attracts fish, which are then speared.

The famous BirdsEye fish fingers were first produced in 1955 at the BirdsEye factory in Great Yarmouth, UK.

A very cool invention

There was lots of work to be done. Clarence had to come up with ways to prepare, store, and package the frozen food — from building machines that filleted the fish, to creating waterproof ink to use on the boxes. Eventually, Clarence patented an invention in 1924 that revolutionized frozen food production — the multiple plate freezer. This was a machine that packed meat or vegetables into cartons, which were then squeezed between two freezing metal plates, creating smaller ice crystals than other techniques, and chilling the food more quickly.

Later that year, BirdsEye products appeared in shops for the first time. These included familiar frozen foods that you can see today, such as fish fillets and raspberries, as well as more unusual products like oysters! As more people bought freezers, and cold train cars were built to transport the goods around the country, the frozen food industry boomed. In 1924, one of Clarence's early businesses went bankrupt, but within just five years, he'd sold his very successful frozen food company, General Seafood Corporation, for the modern equivalent of around $250 million.

LIZZIE MAGIE

American game designer
1886–1948

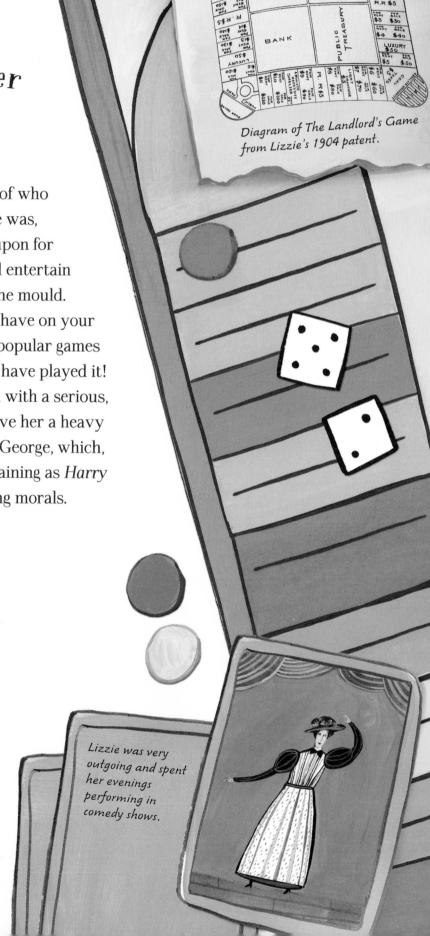

Diagram of The Landlord's Game from Lizzie's 1904 patent.

How many inventors can you think of who are also stand-up comics? Lizzie Magie was, 100 years ago! Back then, it was frowned upon for young American women to go on stage and entertain people by telling jokes — but Lizzie broke the mould. She invented a board game that you might have on your shelf at home — it became one of the most popular games in the world. More than one billion people have played it!

As a child, Lizzie was a serious little girl with a serious, political father. At 12 years old, her dad gave her a heavy book called *Progress and Poverty* by Henry George, which, while not *quite* as entertaining as *Harry Potter*, encouraged strong morals.

In his 1897 book *Progress and Poverty*, Henry George wrote that land belongs to everybody, and no one should be able to make money from it. This inspired Lizzie's board game.

Lizzie was very outgoing and spent her evenings performing in comedy shows.

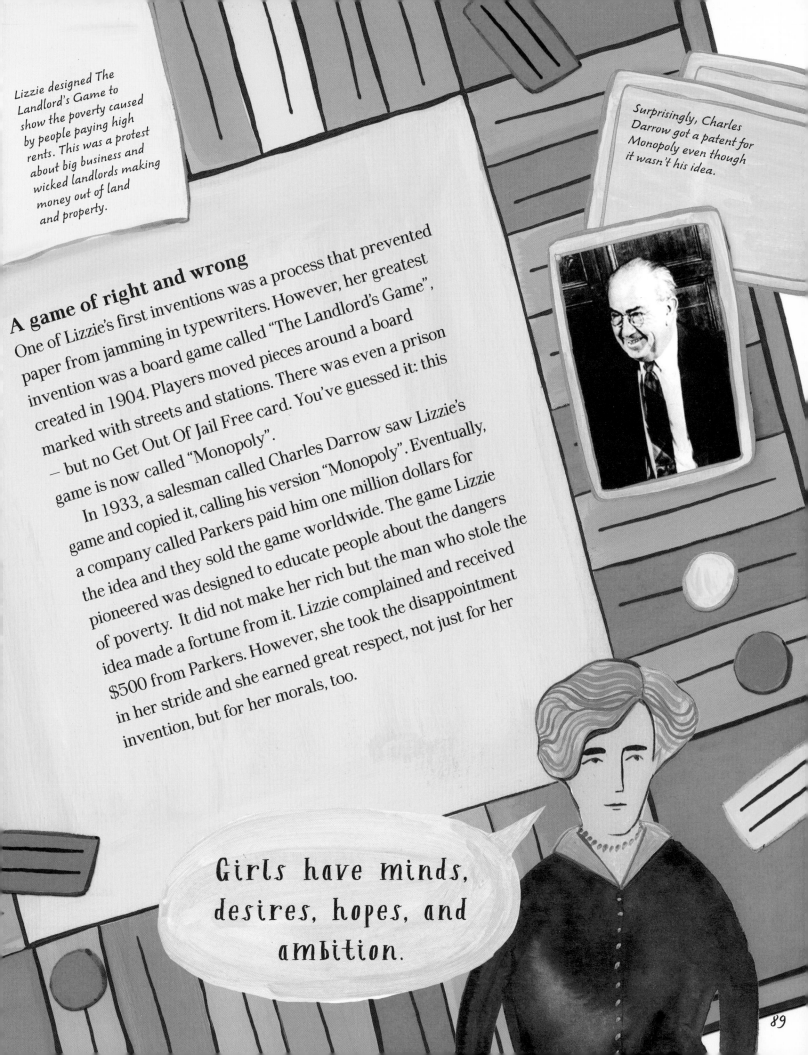

Lizzie designed The Landlord's Game to show the poverty caused by people paying high rents. This was a protest about big business and wicked landlords making money out of land and property.

Surprisingly, Charles Darrow got a patent for Monopoly even though it wasn't his idea.

A game of right and wrong

One of Lizzie's first inventions was a process that prevented paper from jamming in typewriters. However, her greatest invention was a board game called "The Landlord's Game", created in 1904. Players moved pieces around a board marked with streets and stations. There was even a prison – but no Get Out Of Jail Free card. You've guessed it: this game is now called "Monopoly".

In 1933, a salesman called Charles Darrow saw Lizzie's game and copied it, calling his version "Monopoly". Eventually, a company called Parkers paid him one million dollars for the idea and they sold the game worldwide. The game Lizzie pioneered was designed to educate people about the dangers of poverty. It did not make her rich but the man who stole the idea made a fortune from it. Lizzie complained and received $500 from Parkers. However, she took the disappointment in her stride and she earned great respect, not just for her invention, but for her morals, too.

Girls have minds, desires, hopes, and ambition.

89

Winston's Wonders
TOY SHOP

Frisbee

Walter Morrison produced the first plastic flying discs in 1948. The world record distance for throwing one is 338 m (1,108 ft) – beat that!

Tricycle

Stephan Farffler created a three-wheeled wheelchair in the 1600s to help him get around. Today, tricycles are good for young children to ride as they are stable.

Play-Doh

Play-Doh was created when Joseph and Noah McVicker were developing a wallpaper cleaner in 1955. Now, this wonderful flexible plastic can be sculpted into marvellous models!

Do you recognize the toys for sale in this shop? Throughout history, people have created toys for children like you to play with, from the first wooden dolls to the latest video games. The way toys change over time shows what materials were available to their makers. The invention of substances such as plastic have helped bring wacky ideas to life, while developments in technology have helped make clever new creations possible.

Fidget spinner

This addictive spinning toy was probably invented by Catherine Hettinger and took the world by storm in 2017. Some people find that fiddling with it can make them feel more focused and calm.

LEGO®

LEGO® began simply, in the workshop of Danish carpenter Ole Kirk Christiansen, who made play blocks out of wood. He produced the famous plastic bricks in 1949.

Viewmaster

This toy didn't begin as a toy at all – it was originally made by William Gruber in 1938 for adults to look at 3D pictures. It allows you to view small photographs called slides.

Rubik's Cube

Ernö Rubik invented this cube in 1974, supposedly as a way to help his architecture students think more deeply. The world record time to solve it is under 3.5 seconds!

Slinky

Nudge this coiled spring down some stairs, and it'll use gravity to keep going by itself. Richard James invented it by mistake in 1943, when working on a way to keep equipment steady at sea. His wife, Betty, came up with the name "Slinky".

Game Boy

A team led by Satoru Okada and Gunpei Yokoi invented this handheld computer for playing video games in 1989. It was amazingly successful – within 15 years Nintendo had sold more than 200 million of them.

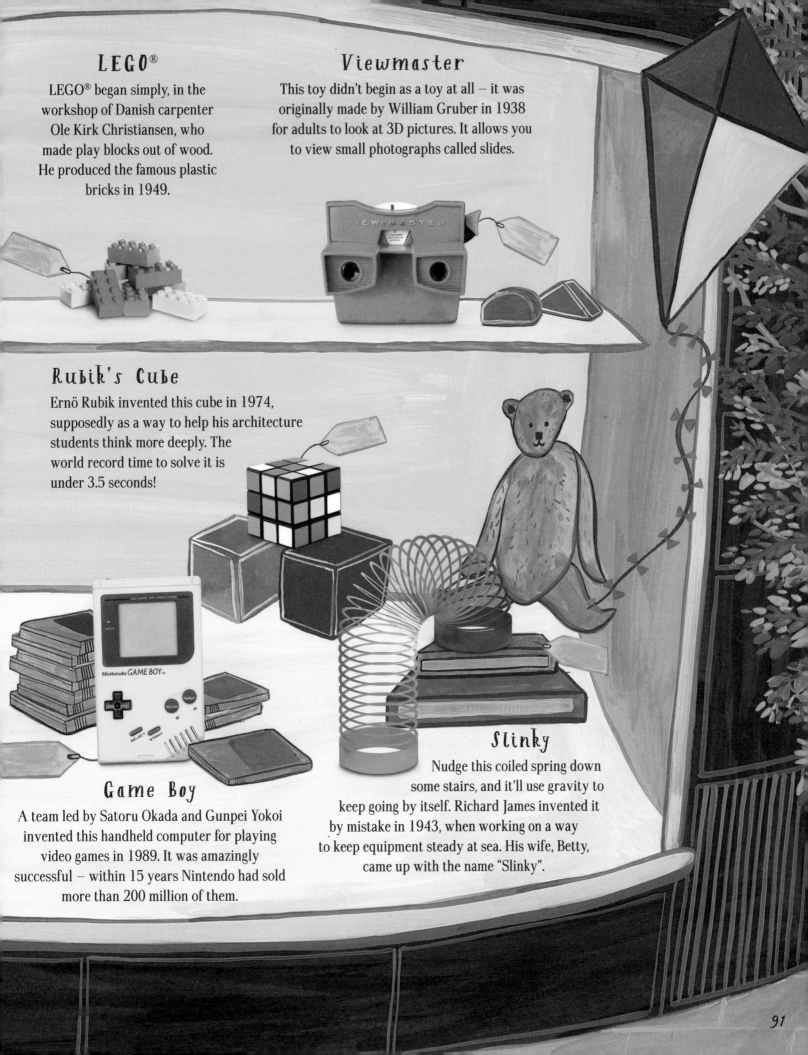

Annie Turnbo Malone was the tenth of eleven children, born on a farm in Illinois, USA, to parents who had been enslaved. Sadly, her mother and father died when she was young. While she was growing up, Annie loved to style her sisters' hair. Although she didn't finish high school, Annie developed a talent for chemistry, which she put to use by experimenting with hair-styling concoctions. This passion would lead to her becoming one of the first female African-American millionaires.

Historically, the long, straight hair of white people was seen as the preferred beauty standard for women's hair. Even after slavery was abolished, this beauty ideal remained in many people's minds, and some African-American women felt pressure to try to straighten their hair. To achieve this they often used treatments like goose fat which damaged their hair and scalps. Annie developed a range of safe products for black hair and went out to sell them door to door. As Annie's business grew, she opened up a factory. Inside, there was also a shop that sold her products and a beauty school, called Poro College. Eventually, she became so successful that she employed more than 200 people.

These daughters of former enslaved people changed the lives of black women around the world.

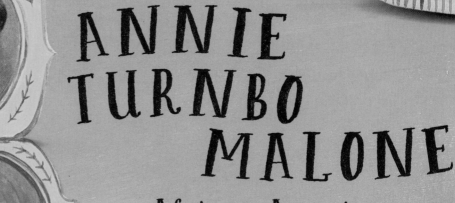

ANNIE TURNBO MALONE
African–American entrepreneur
1877–1957

Sarah Breedlove was one of the people that Annie employed. Like Annie, Sarah's parents were also former slaves who died when she was young. Sarah worked as a child servant, then got married when she was 14, possibly to escape her cruel brother-in-law. Six years later, she was widowed with a young daughter. She moved to St. Louis, washing clothes for a living before eventually taking a job selling beauty products for Annie Turnbo Malone.

Sarah, like many black women of the time, suffered from baldness and infections caused by harsh hair products. She began developing different formulas to help cure her scalp ailments. She learned basic chemistry when she got work as a cook for a pharmacist and created an ointment that cured dandruff. In 1905, she began selling her own brand of hair products under her new name, Madam C. J. Walker, having married Charles Joseph Walker.

Madam Walker remains a household name to this day. Like Annie, she set up her own beauty school. Both women became very wealthy and gave a lot of money to charities and organizations that supported the black community. Their legacies live on.

In her time, Madam Walker was thought to be the richest self-made businesswoman in the USA and owned several cars.

MADAM
C. J. WALKER
African-American
entrepreneur
1867–1919

JOHN LOGIE BAIRD

Scottish engineer 1888–1946

John was a born inventor who was used to failure. His childhood bedroom was littered with unsuccessful inventions like a glass razor that shattered into pieces, and pneumatic (air-operated) shoes that kept bursting. When he tried to make diamonds in his twenties, John caused Glasgow's electricity supply to completely switch off!

First television transmitter

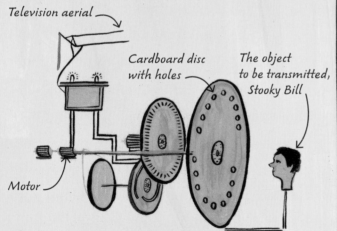

Television aerial

Cardboard disc with holes

The object to be transmitted, Stooky Bill

Motor

Makeshift television

John's first television was made using a hat box, knitting needles, old scissors, bicycle lamp lenses, a large wooden tea chest, and wax. It had a spinning cardboard disc with holes in it, which would each scan different parts of the image to be transmitted. The first image to be transmitted was of a dummy's head that he called Stooky Bill.

John's first public demonstration of a moving image was of this ventriloquist's dummy, which was called "Stooky Bill".

However, John's failure as a child did not affect his determination to succeed as an adult. An inventor who is now known around the world, John was a pioneer of the television. Fascinated with television science since 1903, John set out to do what nobody had done before and exhibit a working television. He built his first television set in 1923, and it was made out of objects that could be found around the home. By 1924, it could transmit, or send, a photographic image to another location 3 m (10 ft) away.

Even though John built his first television successfully, he'd run into issues when making it. He received a massive electric shock and badly burned his hand. Eventually, John's landlord threw him out of his home because he thought his inventions were a fire risk.

Life in colour

A year after he built his first television, John made improvements to its camera. It could now take 12 pictures every second. It wasn't perfect, but it showed clear final images. Then, in 1928, John did something spectacular – he successfully transmitted a colour film of an actress wearing different coloured hats. John also sent television pictures 705 km (438 miles) from London to Glasgow using telephone lines.

This was one of the first images transmitted by John's television. It may have been blurry, but it was an incredible achievement.

John's first television sets looked very different to the ones we have today. They could be extremely heavy and bulky.

John was eventually able to produce high-definition television, which had pictures that are almost as clear as we have now. Sadly, much of John's television equipment was destroyed by a fire just before World War II broke out. John died in 1946, and didn't live long enough to see the incredible televisions we have today. However, he will forever be known as one of the most innovative minds behind television's creation.

Journey through the inventions factory... can you hear the humming and hammering of machines being made? From the fireworks of ancient China, to the robots of today — tools and gadgets have helped to make our lives easier and safer. Meet the geniuses behind mighty machines and terrific technology.

ARCHIMEDES

Greek mathematician
c.287–212 BCE

Archimedes leaped from his bath and ran naked through the streets — or so the story goes. King Hiero had suspected that his crown was not made of pure gold, and had ordered Archimedes, one of the greatest mathematical minds of all time, to investigate. The philosopher was pondering the problem while climbing into a bath, and noticed that the water level rose by an amount equal to his body's volume — the space it takes up. He realized that by submerging the crown, he could measure its volume, and therefore calculate how dense it was. This would reveal whether it was made of pure gold, which is very dense. He was so excited with his discovery that he jumped out of the bath, shouting "Eureka!", which means "I've found it!"

EUREKA!

Water is pulled up through the screw.

Archimedes' screw

The water screw is Archimedes' most famous invention. He came up with it as a way to remove water leaking into ships. This cylinder with a screw inside pulls water up a pipe when rotated. More than 2,000 years later, screws similar to this are still used in farming.

Roman rivals

Archimedes' home city of Syracuse, Sicily, was often threatened by war and Archimedes decided to dedicate the final part of his life to protecting it. In 214 BCE, the Roman army surrounded Syracuse and began a siege that would last several years. Archimedes designed catapults that could throw large rocks at invaders, and giant cranes that would hook onto ships to capsize them. He also built curved mirrors that focused heat and light on enemy ships. It's unlikely that these could have set the ships on fire, but they certainly would have dazzled the sailors and made it more difficult for them to see.

Modern scientists think it's unlikely that Archimedes' "heat ray" would have caused ships to catch fire.

Despite Archimedes' best efforts, the Romans eventually stormed the city. Legend has it that a Roman soldier found Archimedes drawing mathematical diagrams in the sand. Archimedes asked the soldier not to tread on his work, but the solider drew his sword and killed him. This story may not be completely true, but we do know that the Roman general was so upset that a great genius had been murdered, he vowed not to take anything from Syracuse — except, that is, for two models made by Archimedes.

Archimedes was able to prove that the king's crown was not made of pure gold.

The Archimedes Palimpsest revealed work by Archimedes that had been concealed by other writing.

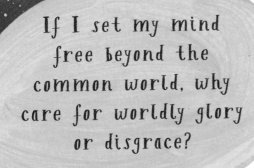

If I set my mind free beyond the common world, why care for worldly glory or disgrace?

ZHANG HENG

Chinese astronomer, mathematician, and poet
78CE–139CE

Zhang Heng was born during the height of ancient China's "Golden Age". This period — the Han Dynasty — saw China enter the world stage as a major power, with rapid progress in trade, science, and technology. Heng's family was well-respected, but not rich. His childhood was tainted by loss, as his dad died when Heng was young.

Leaving home aged 17, Heng had dreams of becoming a writer. He dedicated the next 10 years of his life to studying literature, becoming a highly accomplished poet. However, that was not the full extent of Heng's talents. At the age of 30, he turned his hand to mathematics and science, and soon became well-known for his scientific writings, too. Word of his achievements reached the Imperial Court, and he was summoned to join it. It wasn't long before he was promoted to the prestigious position of chief astronomer.

Heng invented the first ever water-powered armillary sphere — a model which shows how planets rotate in relation to the stars.

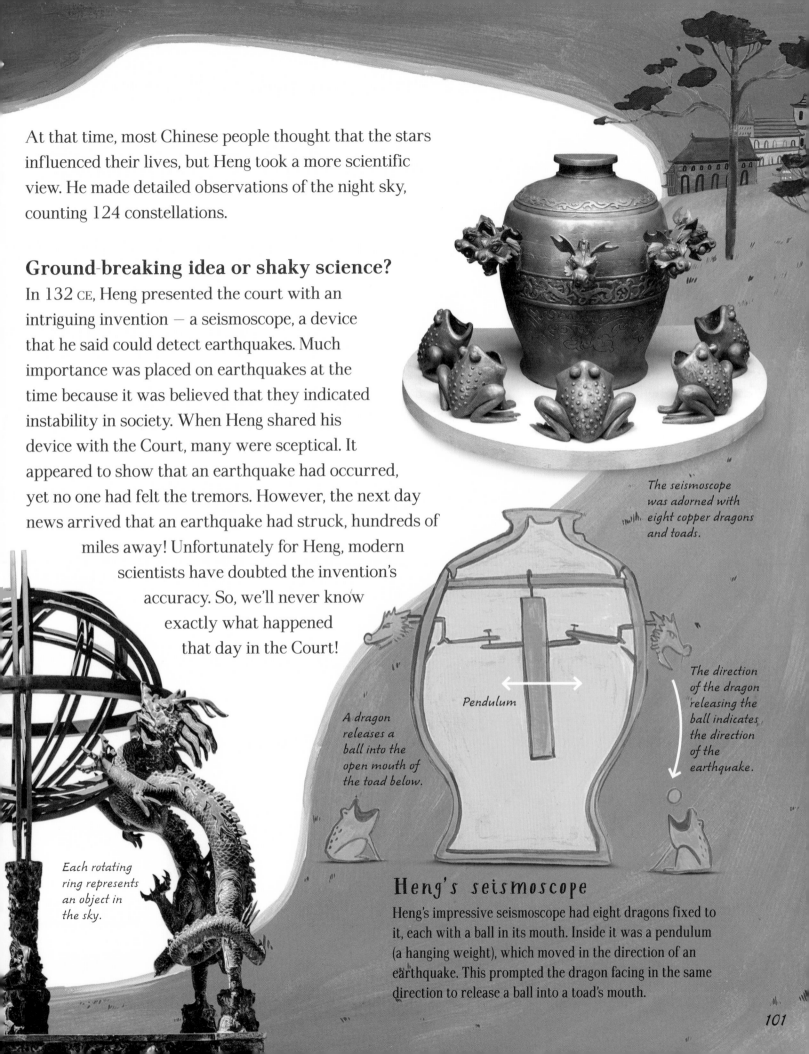

At that time, most Chinese people thought that the stars influenced their lives, but Heng took a more scientific view. He made detailed observations of the night sky, counting 124 constellations.

Ground-breaking idea or shaky science?

In 132 CE, Heng presented the court with an intriguing invention — a seismoscope, a device that he said could detect earthquakes. Much importance was placed on earthquakes at the time because it was believed that they indicated instability in society. When Heng shared his device with the Court, many were sceptical. It appeared to show that an earthquake had occurred, yet no one had felt the tremors. However, the next day news arrived that an earthquake had struck, hundreds of miles away! Unfortunately for Heng, modern scientists have doubted the invention's accuracy. So, we'll never know exactly what happened that day in the Court!

The seismoscope was adorned with eight copper dragons and toads.

Pendulum

A dragon releases a ball into the open mouth of the toad below.

The direction of the dragon releasing the ball indicates the direction of the earthquake.

Each rotating ring represents an object in the sky.

Heng's seismoscope

Heng's impressive seismoscope had eight dragons fixed to it, each with a ball in its mouth. Inside it was a pendulum (a hanging weight), which moved in the direction of an earthquake. This prompted the dragon facing in the same direction to release a ball into a toad's mouth.

LI TIAN
Chinese monk
9th century

It seems amazing that a peace-loving person such as a monk could invent fireworks. However, roughly 1,000 years ago, during the Song Dynasty, it is said that a Chinese monk named Li Tian did just that. Tian lived in the city of Liuyang in Hunan Province, central China. Little is known about his life or why he decided to mix together the ingredients that make firecrackers, an early type of firework. Perhaps he wanted to wake up the other monks! He mixed together charcoal with sulphur and saltpetre (a chemical also known as potassium nitrate) and put them into a hollow bamboo tube. When the end of the tube was set alight, there would have been a loud fizzing sound, followed by an explosion. Maybe he stood well back, but possibly Tian singed his eyebrows or burned his fingers. Whatever happened, you can bet he got a shock!

Chinese people decorate their homes with firecrackers like these to celebrate the new year.

Saltpetre

Charcoal

Bamboo tubes

Sulphur

Fireworks

Today, fireworks are used in celebrations around the world, and Liuyang is the largest producer of them. But remember, this mixture of charcoal, sulphur, and saltpetre is not something you should try to make at home. It creates gunpowder, which is used by builders to blow up rocks.

The dragon is a symbol of strength and power in Chinese culture.

Legend has it...

One story says Tian invented firecrackers because he was threatened by the spirit of a fierce dragon with big claws and sharp teeth. The legend goes that he shot the firecrackers at the dragon as a way to rid the town of its evil spirit. The loud bang scared the dragon so much, it never returned.

Another tale tells of an evil spirit causing floods in Hunan Province, that only ended after Tian let off an explosion.

Chinese people celebrate the invention of firecrackers each year on 18 April. There is even a special shrine to Tian in the Fireworks Museum in Liuyang. We may never know the truth behind Tian's story or how fireworks were invented, but it certainly gives you something to ponder next time you gaze up at dazzling displays in the sky.

ISMAIL AL-JAZARI

Turkish engineer and artist
1136–1206

Ismail created designs for raising and pumping water.

When do you think robots were first invented? As far back as 900 years ago, Abu al-Iz Ibn Ismail ibn al-Razaz al-Jazari (Ismail al-Jazari for short) created hundreds of amazing designs for robots in his book, *The Book of Knowledge and Ingenious Mechanical Devices*. A man of many talents — a mathematician, artist, astronomer, and engineer — Ismail al-Jazari and his marvellous mechanical designs were years ahead of their time.

A reproduction of Ismail's castle clock, complete with robot musicians, stood 3.5 m (11 ft) high.

Ismail was born in Mesopotamia (in modern-day Turkey). Growing up, it's likely that he learned about science from his dad, who was an engineer at the Artukid Palace in Diyarbakır, before following in his footsteps and taking a position there himself in 1174. Ismail rose up the ranks to become the Palace's chief engineer. His favourite part of the job was making things — he considered himself a craftsman — and he had many imaginative ideas for mechanical devices.

The elephant clock

Ismail's elaborate 6.7 m (22 ft) tall elephant clock could be said to be an early example of a robot design. The clock was driven by a tank of water hidden inside the elephant, which caused other elements to move or make a noise.

The mechanism caused the bird to whistle, a bit like a cuckoo clock.

Each part of the clock represents a different culture that influenced Ismail, including Indian, African, Chinese, Persian, Greek, and Islamic cultures.

The man struck a cymbal every half an hour.

Islamic Golden Age

Ismail al-Jazari lived during the height of the Islamic Golden Age — a time when advances in science, technology, and engineering flourished across the Islamic world.

Amazing automata

Prince Nasir al-Din Mahmud convinced Ismail to write his book, which became an early encyclopedia of engineering.

An elephant model powering a clock, a peacock pouring water, and a robot waitress serving tea are just some of the weird and wonderful features of Ismail's designs. Automata (moving mechanical devices) appealed to the prince, so Ismail included lots of them. These clever mechanisms were extremely complex for the time, and there is even a description of the first suction pump. Writing this book was a labour of love for Ismail, who dedicated years of his life to it — only finishing it a few months before his death in 1206. Ismail's book remains one of the most impressive achievements of the Islamic Golden Age.

JOHANNES GUTENBERG

German craftsperson and publisher • 1398–1468

Johannes Gutenberg changed the world more than almost any other inventor. Printing is one of the most important and influential inventions in history. Humans have been on Earth for more than 100,000 years, but we only learned to write 4,000 years ago. When books were first invented 3,000 years ago, a scribe needed to write them by hand using a special ink and pen on parchment, which was made from the dried skin of a dead animal.

One single book used to take as long as a year to finish, with one page taking more than a day to write. However, Johannes revolutionized this process with his invention of the printing press just 550 years ago. With this machine, he could print 250 pages every hour!

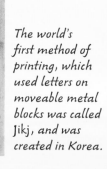

The world's first method of printing, which used letters on moveable metal blocks was called Jikj, and was created in Korea.

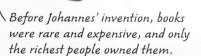

Before Johannes' invention, books were rare and expensive, and only the richest people owned them.

Just his type

Johannes came from Mainz, Germany, and lived near the River Rhine, where wine and oil industries were important. The heavy printing press, which screwed down paper with great force onto metal blocks, was very similar to wine or olive presses. People had tried printing with carved, wooden blocks, but they weren't as strong as metal. It had to be melted down to make the blocks, which meant that metalwork skills were essential, so it's likely that Johannes was a trained goldsmith — a person who makes objects out of gold.

The most famous book that Johannes published was the Bible. It was partly printed and partly decorated by hand. More than 40 copies are still around today — each worth millions of pounds.

A spring of truth shall flow from it: like a new star it shall scatter the darkness of ignorance.

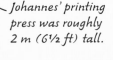

Johannes' printing press was roughly 2 m (6½ ft) tall.

The printing press

Johannes' machine produced sharp and clear printed pages because it used smooth, hard-edged metal blocks. Each individual letter could be moved around to be used again and again, to print any word with great accuracy.

Johannes knew that his printing press would mean that books would become more affordable, and more people could buy them. Within 40 years of his death, there were more than 1,000 printing presses in Europe. Printing led to improved education and the rapid spread of information and news. By the 1800s, printing presses were powered by engines, and modern models can print up to 100,000 pages an hour!

SYBILLA RIGHTON MASTERS

American inventor • c.1676–1720

Sybilla was the first American to receive an English patent for her invention. The cornmeal (ground-up corn) produced from her corn mill, devised more than 300 years ago, is still eaten in the USA today. Sybilla's parents were Quakers — Christians who believe in living simply. In the early 1690s, she married Thomas Masters, a wealthy Quaker landowner, and had four children — Mary, Sarah, Thomas, and William.

Sybilla's invention was inspired by watching Native American women grind corn. They used wooden poles to pound the corn kernels, resulting in a gritty texture. Sybilla devised a water-powered machine that used hammers to stamp on the corn, eliminating the hard work of doing it by hand. She called the product "Tuscarora Rice", but today it is known as grits.

Crossing the Atlantic Ocean was dangerous — there was risk of storms and pirate attacks!

To patent her invention, Sybilla needed to apply to the British government, who ruled America at this time. Boldly, she decided to travel to London, leaving her family behind. Back then, it was very unusual for a woman to travel by herself. When she arrived, she learned that only the monarch could grant patents, and her application was initially rejected. After nearly three years, in 1715 King George I finally approved Sybilla's patent. However, married women were not allowed to patent inventions themselves, so her husband, Thomas, signed the application.

Some old mills in the USA are still in operation, while others have been turned into museums.

While she was waiting for her patents to be approved, Sybilla opened a successful shop in London, selling hats and bonnets.

After receiving a second patent from King George, for a new method of hat-making using palmetto leaf, Sybilla went home. The Masters opened a mill to produce Tuscarora Rice, hoping to sell it in London, but it was not popular. To try to increase sales, they even told people it was a cure for illness, which was completely untrue! Although grits never sold well in London, they are still regularly eaten for breakfast in the USA.

Water flowed over a big wheel outside the mill, turning it and powering the machinery.

Heavy hammers dropped onto the corn, pounding it into cornmeal. It then went into shallow trays to dry.

CHARLES BABBAGE
British mathematician
1791–1871

Charles Babbage was a bright but sickly boy, who almost died of fever when he was eight. Often too ill for school, he studied at home and got to learn about what interested him most — maths. He grew up to become a man with many gifts: he was rich, had good looks, famous friends, and studied at Cambridge University, becoming a professor, but never giving a lecture!

Charles was so clever that he designed the first-ever computers. In his time, people worked out calculations by themselves, which led to errors that could have serious consequences, such as ships becoming stranded due to navigation mistakes. Charles wanted to replace people with the steam-driven machines that he designed: the "Difference Engine" and then, later, the "Analytical Engine", which would complete more difficult calculations. However, his designs were complex and very expensive to build — a working model wouldn't be completed for 150 years!

Charles became increasingly grumpy in old age. His beloved wife died very young as did three of his children. This, together with the failure of his most ambitious plans, led to frustration and sadness.

There is a smaller version of the Analytical Engine, now finally working, in London's Science Museum.

The Analytical Engine

Charles' computer was designed to solve tricky calculations and store information. A series of cards with holes would be fed into the machine to tell it what to do.

ADA LOVELACE
British mathematician
1815–1852

Ada Lovelace was a lively little girl, born into a famous family. Her father, the poet Lord Byron, had many lovers and left his wife within weeks of Ada's birth. Lady Byron did not want Ada to become a poet like her dad, so made her follow strict rules and study intensely. Ada worked hard, but never lost her creativity, writing a book when she was 12 called *Flyology*, with designs for a winged flying machine.

Ada was 17 when she met Charles Babbage at a party. They got on very well, Charles calling her "Lady Fairy" because of her fascination with flying. He was impressed by her mathematical skill and Ada was excited by his ideas of a calculation engine.

Lady Byron loved maths. Lord Byron called her "the princess of parallelograms".

Ada wrote to Charles to explain that the Analytical Engine could be programmed.

Number cruncher

The Italian mathematician Luigi Menabrea published a paper about Charles' Analytical Engine, which Ada translated and expanded. It seems Ada, rather than Charles, understood that machines might do tasks far beyond counting numbers — they had potential to write secret codes or compose music. This is why she is often regarded as the first computer programmer. Sadly, Ada died young and the music she imagined a computer creating wouldn't sound for a hundred years.

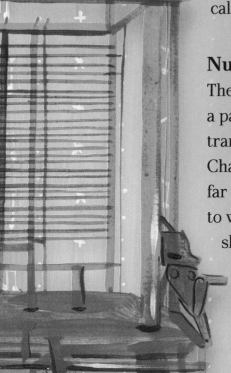

ELISHA OTIS

American carpenter and engineer
1811–1861

E lisha Otis' luck went up and down throughout his life, but his invention transformed the way cities are built. He grew up in Vermont, USA, and moved back and forth between there and New York, dabbling in jobs as a wagon driver and builder, a carpenter, and also running a sawmill. He was never very successful and his life was marked by misfortune.

When his wife Susan suddenly died, he found himself poor and left with a small boy and a baby in nappies.

Desperate to support his young family, Elisha tried to make a fresh start as a doll-maker. When this didn't work out, he turned his hand to working as a mechanic for a bed-frame factory, and took to inventing in his spare time. Elisha began creating everything from a brake to be used on trains, to an automatic bread oven. In 1852, he was tasked with turning an abandoned mill into a factory. It was while cleaning it up that he began to wonder how to move heavy objects between floors. He was struck by an idea that meant his prospects would finally be going up.

> All safe, gentlemen, all safe.

Elisha's assistant cut the cable holding up the platform.

The platform rested on notches along the side.

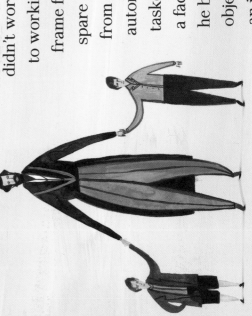

Elisha's sons, Charles and Norton, would one day take over the family business.

The safety elevator

Old hoisting platforms were unsafe and the ropes often broke, causing injuries and even deaths. Elisha and his sons designed an elevator with a device that would stop the elevator from crashing down if its cable broke.

Elisha's patent for the safety device used in his elevator was granted in 1852.

A success on so many levels

Elisha designed an elevator, or lift, and began to make them, converting the mill into an elevator factory. At first, sales were few and far between. People were terrified of falling and didn't believe that the safety brake worked. This all changed at the 1854 New York Business Fair. Wearing a top hat, Elisha stood on his high platform and his assistant cut the cable holding it up. People gasped as the platform began to drop. Then they saw that the safety catch worked – Elisha was right! Bowing to the crowd, he removed his hat with a dignified flourish and said, "All safe, gentlemen, all safe".

Have you seen a skyscraper before? We've got Elisha to thank for them. When he was alive, not many buildings were more than four storeys high, as you had to climb the stairs. Elisha designed a steam engine to power his elevators, which meant architects were able to build much taller buildings. Elisha was a terrible businessman, and died in debt despite his world-changing invention. However, after his death, his two loving sons managed the Otis Elevator Company wisely, and it became hugely successful.

An Otis elevator was installed into the Eiffel Tower, in Paris, in 1889.

ALFRED NOBEL
Swedish chemist and engineer
1833–1896

Alfred Nobel's interest in explosives was ignited at an early age. His inventor father taught him the basics, although the elder Nobel failed to make much money from his work himself, and Alfred's family were poor. Of his seven brothers and sisters, four died as children. After a string of failures, Alfred's dad eventually invented an underwater mine, an explosive used to sink ships, and the Nobels' luck began to change. They became very wealthy and could afford to send Alfred to the best schools, where he excelled at chemistry and languages. Alfred went on to study in France and the USA, and his passion for explosives burned more and more brightly. Returning to Sweden, he began work on the explosive nitroglycerine. He was trying to make it safe, so that it wouldn't blow up unexpectedly when pressed or heated. This led to several serious accidents, so the government banned such experiments within the city. Undeterred, Alfred moved his base to a boat on a nearby lake. Eventually he developed the invention he is most famous for — dynamite, a much safer alternative to nitroglycerine. Sadly, he only perfected it after his brother Emil died in a nitroglycerine explosion.

Alfred created dynamite by mixing nitroglycerine with a fine sand called kieselguhr.

Alfred patented dynamite in 1866, and it was much in demand from the construction industry.

Alfred demonstrated the effects of dynamite at Lake Mälaren near Stockholm, Sweden where his boat was moored.

Alfred went on to patent a whopping 355 inventions and owned 90 weapon-making factories. He also invented gelignite, which was an even more powerful explosive than dynamite, as well as ballistite, a smokeless explosive that was used in bullets. He became famous as a millionaire manufacturer of explosives.

Legacy of destruction or kindness?

In 1888, Alfred's brother Ludwig died suddenly while on holiday in France, but the newspapers thought it was the famous Alfred Nobel who had died. The story goes that they published criticisms of Alfred because his inventions caused harm. Alfred is said to have read the newspapers and felt devastated. He did not want his legacy to be that of death and destruction and was so ashamed that he vowed to leave his millions to charity. And so the Nobel Prizes were founded, which are given each year to people who have made a difference in the world. Many such people are included in this very book.

Alfred's will stated that he would leave all his money to charity.

The Nobel Prize

The Nobel Prize charity was set up in Alfred's name. The prizes are given each year to people making major advances in chemistry, physics, medicine, literature, and to those promoting peace.

Nobel Prize medal

WEIRD, WONDERFUL,

Some inventors have come up with ideas so bizarre, you'd think they'd gone mad. However, whether they were years ahead of their time or their creations were a complete failure, you can't say that the people behind these inventions lacked imagination!

Moustache cup — wonderful!

There are still eccentric men who spend hours waxing their moustaches into extraordinary shapes. In the 1870s, Harvey Adams patented this cup with a little shelf inside to stop his moustache from getting wet.

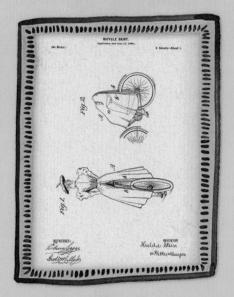

The shelf hidden inside the mug had a hole to drink through.

Perpetual motion machine — impossible!

Many inventors have tried to build machines that move eternally by themselves. It's impossible, because motion requires energy, and machines can't generate any on their own.

In 1807, Thomas Young designed this device to turn by itself, but it didn't work.

Egg cuber — impossible!

Stan Pargman invented this device to cook square eggs in 1976. The idea was to stop eggs rolling off the plate, but unfortunately they still slid around!

The Square Egg Company was established in Los Angeles, USA.

Bicycle skirt — wonderful!

Hulda Stein designed this skirt in 1898 to make it easier for women to cycle. It wasn't an idea that caught on, although it may have become caught up in the chain!

Umbrella hat — weird!

Invented by Robert Patten in 1880, this hat protects you from the Sun and the rain. Australians have been known to wear them at cricket matches!

Doggles — wonderful!

These might look like old-fashioned pilot goggles, but dogs don't fly aeroplanes! These glasses protect against sunlight and help short-sighted dogs to see bones that are far away.

Fish-tank toilet — weird!

A company called Runto Sanitary Ware invented this three-tank toilet in China in 2008. One tank is for water flowing in, one is for water draining out, and a third is for fish — hopefully, you don't flush the wrong tank!

In memoriam

Not all inventions are successful. These three risk-takers sadly died at the hands of their own inventions. The memories of them live on.

Inventor of the coat parachute, Franz Reichelt died when he jumped from the Eiffel Tower in 1912. Unfortunately, his invention couldn't slow his fall.

In the 1600s, Wan Hu attached 47 rockets to a chair. He tried to fly to the Moon, but only achieved a big bang and a burning smell. There is a crater on the Moon named after him.

Abu Nasir Ismail jumped from a roof and tried to fly using wooden wings in 1008 CE. Sadly, he fell rather than flew.

MARGARET ELOISE KNIGHT

American inventor
1838–1914

Paper bags are used by millions of people every single day, but did you know that they were developed by an 18-year-old? Margaret, or Mattie, had always enjoyed fixing things. As a child, she used tools to improve her brothers' toys, and even made kites and sledges.

The metal safety guard Mattie invented helped to protect children working in textile mills.

When Mattie's father died, she had to earn money for her family. At just 12 years old, she began working in a textile mill, making cloth, instead of going to school. The mill was a dangerous place — Mattie had only been there about one month when she witnessed a terrifying accident. A piece of weaving equipment called a shuttle flew off a cloth-weaving machine and injured one of the workers. Mattie built a metal safety guard to stop this happening again.

Mattie's bags fold down flat.

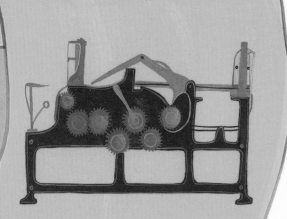

Mattie's machine

Made out of wood, and then later, iron, this paper bag-making machine was a huge success. It not only folded the bags into the correct shape, but also glued them together. Automating the process saved lots of time, and thousands of versions of this machine are still used today.

A big idea for a simple product

At 18, Mattie began working at the Columbia Paper Bag factory in Massachusetts, USA. It was here that she saw how useless their paper bags were. Shaped like envelopes, the bags couldn't carry much at all. Mattie realized that to improve the design, paper bags needed square, flat bottoms. These bags would be able to stand upright without support and could hold much more weight. Mattie began making them by hand, but this took a lot of time.

She spent two years designing a marvellous machine that would make the bags, and when she'd perfected it, Mattie applied for a patent. However, she discovered that a man named Charles Annan had been spying on her in the factory and had stolen her idea! He'd even been granted a patent for the design. Determined to prove that the idea was hers, Mattie gathered her drawings, took Charles to court, and won! Finally, she owned the rights to her machine and could sell her bags to stores all around the USA.

Mattie's inventive streak did not stop there. She went on to patent more than 25 inventions and create many more successful products — shoemaking machines, sewing equipment, and car engines to name a few.

Mattie named her creation the "Bag Machine".

Today, flat-bottomed paper bags are used in food stores around the world.

HERTHA AYRTON

British mathematician and scientist
1854–1923

Hertha rose from humble beginnings to become one of the most influential British scientists in history. Her father was a Polish immigrant who struggled to make enough money for his family. He died when Hertha was only seven, and his wife, a seamstress, was left to look after their eight children. As a child, Hertha attended a school run by two of her aunts. It was there that her exceptional mathematical ability became clear.

While at Cambridge University, Hertha formed a women's fire brigade. They practised climbing ladders in long skirts.

At just 16 years old, Hertha began tutoring to earn money for the family. Her friends and family could see how intelligent she was, and persuaded her to apply to study at Cambridge University. Hertha passed the entrance exam with flying colours, and began a maths course.

It was at Cambridge that Hertha built her first inventions — a blood-pressure monitor that counted heartbeats and a mathematical measuring device.

Hertha lit the way for future female inventors.

Hertha was one of the first women to show off her inventions at the Institution of Electrical Engineers.

Hertha's searchlights were used at night to identify enemy aircraft during World War I.

A light in the dark

At the time when Hertha was at Cambridge University, women could only receive a certificate for studying, which was not as highly recognized as a degree. Determined to prove her worth as a mathematician, Hertha also studied at the University of London, where she finally gained a degree in 1881. Four years later, she married William Ayrton, an electrical engineer.

Alongside William, Hertha worked on many inventions — most importantly electric arc lamps. These were used to make bright street lights and military searchlights, as well as lights for projecting films. However, there was a problem — they made a rather frightening hissing noise, like a snake! People were afraid of using them, until Hertha put a stop to the noise — she realized that if the lamps were air-tight, they would not make the strange sound.

Hertha made significant contributions to the world of science, but as a woman, she had to fight for recognition. She was a supporter of the suffragettes, a group that fought for women's rights. In 1919, Hertha founded the International Federation of University Women. Hertha's story has inspired women around the world to see that they, too, can be successful scientists.

Hertha also invented a special fan that could blow away poisonous gas, for soldiers to use in World War I.

Without a proper laboratory, Hertha built many of her inventions at home.

NIKOLA TESLA
Serbian–American electrical and mechanical engineer
1856–1943

According to family legend, Nikola was born at midnight as a massive thunderstorm raged outside. The terrified nurse delivering him worried that this was a bad omen and Nikola would be a baby of storm. "No," said his mother, as lightning struck, "he will be a baby of light."

As a teenager, Nikola became very ill and his father, a priest, promised that if he recovered he could go to a top school. Luckily, Nikola got better and so he set off to study engineering in Austria. In 1884, Nikola moved to the USA to work at Edison Machine Works, fixing electricity generators. However, after six months he quit and set up his own company. Several of his businesses failed, but Nikola persevered and, in 1887, invented one of the first induction motors. It generated electricity using magnetic fields — invisible forces that push and pull around magnets.

Nikola's mum was always inventing ingenious new tools for use around the house.

At school, Nikola learned about Niagara Falls and imagined generating power from the rushing water.

One day, I will harness that power.

The induction motor

Nikola's invention was a simple self-starting machine that didn't need regular repairing like previous electric motors. It used alternating current (AC), which allows large amounts of electricity to be transmitted efficiently over long distances. Today, AC powers homes around the world.

Nikola loved teasing people. Newspapers published edited images of him surrounded by lightning from the Tesla coil.

Niagara Falls lies on the border between Canada and the USA.

A shocking turn of events

Over the next decade, Nikola astounded the world with his inventions. In 1889, he invented the Tesla coil, which transforms a weak electric charge into a more powerful one. In his Colorado Springs laboratory, Nikola demonstrated a massive coil that produced terrifying lightning sparks 40 m (131 ft) long. The noise, like thunder, was equally frightening and the demonstration caused a local power cut. He found that a light bulb held near the Tesla coil would light up spontaneously, even without being connected with wires, and used this trick to amaze crowds. Nikola loved to put on a show. During another demonstration, he made the audience think he was controlling a small boat with his voice, when really he was using radio control.

By the early 1900s, Nikola's money had run dry. He spent his last years in New York, leaving monstrous bills at luxury hotels where he lodged and feeding pigeons in the park. Long after his thunderous birth that stormy night, Nikola Tesla became a true man of light — remembered as a brilliant electrical visionary who was always searching for ways to provide power to the world.

In 1895, Nikola built an electric power plant at Niagara Falls, fulfilling his childhood dream. The Falls now help to power several cities.

Towards the end of his life, Nikola spent a lot of time nursing his favourite pigeon back to health.

LISE MEITNER

Austrian–Swedish physicist • 1878–1968

OTTO HAHN

German chemist 1879–1968

Otto Hahn and Lise Meitner were pen pals with a difference – they were responsible for one of the most important scientific developments of the 20th century. However, it wasn't easy – their unique skills and ability to work together were put to the test by the rise of Nazi Germany. But let's start at the beginning...

As a young boy, Otto did chemistry experiments in his mother's laundry room. His passion for chemistry took him to work at universities in Frankfurt, Munich, and Berlin in Germany, and Montreal in Canada. It was in Berlin that he first met the Austrian physicist Lise Meitner, who was Jewish and only the second woman awarded a doctorate at Vienna University.

As a woman, Lise was not allowed to work in German university labs. Otto, however, recognized Lise's talent and took her on as an assistant at his makeshift lab in a converted cellar. She quickly progressed alongside him, and by 1926 was appointed as the first female professor in Berlin. However, in 1933 Adolf Hitler came to power in Germany and began persecuting Jewish people. In desperation, Lise fled in 1938. She couldn't take any money, so Otto gave Lise his mother's diamond ring to bribe the border guards between Holland and Germany.

Lise fled from Germany to Sweden, where she became a citizen.

Otto gave Lise a diamond ring to give her a chance to escape Nazi Germany.

Lise eventually made it to Sweden, but this meant she was separated from her work partner. They kept in contact by writing letters to each other. One day, Otto wrote to Lise to tell her that he'd made a discovery — firing tiny particles called neutrons at a substance called uranium produced another substance, called barium.

Otto's table, where he carried out his experiments.

Lise wrote back to say she had worked out what was happening — the neutrons were splitting the atoms of uranium, which also released lots of energy. She called this "nuclear fission".

Together, they had invented a way of creating nuclear energy, which could be used to power homes and create extremely destructive bombs. However, both Otto and Lise opposed their discovery being used as a weapon. In recognition of their efforts, Otto, but not Lise, won a Nobel Prize. Lise was eventually honoured too — the element meitnerium is named after her.

Lise and Otto worked together in this Berlin building for more than 20 years. It was named the Otto Hahn Building until 2010, when it was renamed the Hahn-Meitner Building.

Today, nuclear energy powers many homes.

Nuclear fission

Nuclear fission takes place in atoms — the small building blocks that make up everything. There's a huge amount of energy stored in the nucleus, or centre, of an atom. By firing a neutron at a nucleus you can split the nucleus, releasing the energy.

Neutron

Nucleus

Neutron

Nucleus

Nucleus has split in two

Neutron

Neutron

Neutron

125

LYNN CONWAY

American computer scientist and electrical engineer • 1938–present

One of Lynn's first inventions was a reflecting telescope, which she used to take photos of the Moon.

Lynn was a budding scientist from a young age. Her father was a chemical engineer, and she learned to read from the science book he gave her. She excelled in science and maths at school, and in her free time built creative engineering projects with her brother at their home in Mount Vernon, New York, USA, including a photograph enlarger and a telescope.

When she was 17, Lynn was accepted into the Massachusetts Institute of Technology (MIT), one of the best universities for science, to study physics. By the end of her first year, she was in the top two per cent of students.

Lynn loved to clear her head on long hikes in the mountains, especially on Breakneck Ridge, New York.

After a while, Lynn started to lose interest in her studies, and ended up leaving university because she felt so unhappy. Lynn was struggling — she'd been brought up as a boy, but knew inside that she was a girl. It was difficult to come forward and share her true identity, and when she tried, people didn't understand her. By 1961, Lynn needed a new start and returned home, saving up to go back to college to study computer programming. For a while, she tried again to live as a man, but still felt she was pretending to be someone she was not.

The computer revolution

In 1964, Lynn joined IBM, a big technology company. She performed research on a top-secret project building a high-performance supercomputer. Lynn's insights were vital to the project's success, but when she bravely decided to begin her transition from male to female, she was fired. This was the beginning of some tough years, as Lynn lost family and friends and was rejected from jobs because she was a trans woman. However, she managed to rebuild her career, choosing to keep her past a secret because of the discrimination she'd faced.

During the 1970s, scientists were looking into making smaller computers using electronic chips, so they could be used in cars and household appliances. Together with the engineer Carver Mead, Lynn, now working at PARC electronics lab, published a book that explained how to design electronic chips, enabling students to do it themselves.

During the 1960s, people did not have computers at home. They were mostly used for scientific research at universities and organizations such as NASA.

Lynn's work led to the creation of the Pentium chip, which has been used in millions of computers.

Lynn rose to the top of her profession, working at the US Defence Department's computer research programme and teaching for many years. The system that Lynn had invented when she was at IBM was now a standard for computer design and other people were taking credit for what she'd done. Lynn made the difficult decision to "come out" and tell her story, bringing her accomplishments to light. More recently, she has fought as an activist for the rights of transgender individuals in the workplace. Lynn can now be fully credited as a pioneer in the development of the supercomputer and electronic chip, as well as a role model for young scientists from all backgrounds.

TIM BERNERS-LEE

British software engineer 1955–present

When Tim Berners-Lee first imagined a way of sharing information between computers, he had not the slightest idea that it would change the world.

Tim grew up around computer scientists. Both his parents worked on one of the first computers that people could buy. He began making his own electronic devices to control the model railway that wound around his room. His interest in electronics led him to study physics. He kept tinkering with gadgets alongside his studies, and made his own computer out of the parts from a broken TV set.

After university, he began working as a computer program designer. Sometimes, he'd just lie on his back on a patch of grass and stare at the sky, thinking up solutions to problems he wanted to fix. After a few years, he went to work at CERN in Geneva, Switzerland, where scientists study the particles that make up our universe.

Computers weren't readily available to buy when Tim was young, so he used parts from an old TV set and made his own!

Overview.html

The first websites were all linked from Overview.html

Websites are stored on web servers. This computer was used by Tim at CERN to access the first-ever web server.

http://slacvm.slac.stanford.edu/FIND/default.html

The USA's first server was at Stanford University.

"This is for everyone"

Tim shared this message during the 2012 Olympics, using the website Twitter. He wants everyone to be able to access and use the World Wide Web for free.

World Wide what?

Tim wanted to find an easy way for researchers at CERN to share information with one another on a network called the Internet, using computers. He invented a system called hypertext, which allowed computer users to find out more about something by clicking on a link. The idea of a worldwide system of information, the "World Wide Web", was soon born, and the first web browser was created to link the information. The first website — http://info.cern.ch — launched in August 1991. To help the Internet spread around the world, Tim made his invention free to all.

The World Wide Web is now made up of hundreds of millions of websites, containing huge amounts of information. Anyone who has an internet connection can access and learn from it. It has sometimes been used for bad things, such as spreading false information, but most people wouldn't want to be without Tim's amazing achievement.

OLGA D. GONZÁLEZ-SANABRIA

Puerto Rican scientist
1956–present

Olga grew up in a tiny town called Patillas on the Caribbean island of Puerto Rico. She loved maths and science, but traditionally girls weren't encouraged to study subjects like engineering. She never even remotely thought that one day she might become a space scientist, until she went on an inspirational school trip to a university. Olga went on to study engineering and attained a Master of Science degree.

In 1979, Olga was delighted to be hired by NASA, who were interested in finding new ways to make energy without using coal and other fossil fuels, which take millions of years to form and cause pollution. The challenge of finding ways to reduce the use of fossil fuels and working on the space programme was, she says, "enticing", so she seized the opportunity.

Olga went straight from university to work in NASA's labs.

Keeping the lights on

At NASA, Olga worked on several projects relating to the International Space Station (ISS), home to six astronauts who live and work in space. She was instrumental in developing the Long Cycle-Life Nickel-Hydrogen Batteries that helped power the ISS. The space station has massive solar panels that convert sunlight into electricity. However, space is intensely cold, and as the ISS orbits Earth every 92 minutes, it is in complete darkness 15 times a day — so batteries are essential to store the power that keeps the station running. With her team, Olga worked hard to invent efficient batteries that last a long time, because it's tricky to replace things in space!

The batteries Olga developed are recharged by sunlight falling on solar panels attached to the ISS.

Olga continued to progress at NASA and became Director of Engineering at the Glenn Research Center. There, she developed projects to test how technology would perform in space.

Olga emphasizes that collaboration is essential for success, and has enjoyed mentoring students over the years. As a successful Hispanic engineer who has won many awards for her work, she is a role model for young scientists from diverse backgrounds.

NASA has recently been fitting the ISS with lighter and longer-lasting lithium-ion batteries.

Tesla cars have clever computers inside that can steer the car without a driver. In the future, it's likely that many vehicles will be driverless.

Elon has built tubes to test his Hyperloop idea and plans to open the transport system in California, USA.

The first stage of the Falcon 9 rocket is designed to be able to return to Earth, so it can be reused.

Elon Musk is the inventor with unlimited ambition. His ideas aren't just high-tech — many are designed to help humanity beat the challenges it faces from global warming. He has dedicated his life, and billions of dollars, to making the future a better place.

For most of his childhood, Elon lived with his father, who was separated from his mother. His dad was a brilliant engineer, but he was very busy. Elon spent his time reading piles of books, building rockets, and doing experiments with little supervision.

As a 12-year-old, Elon learned to code and built computer games, which he sold. By the time he had finished university, he was creating companies. One such business allowed people to pay for things online, which is now a very successful website called PayPal. Elon sold his early companies for huge sums, which allowed him to think about even more ambitious projects.

ELON MUSK
South African entrepreneur
1971–present

Elon is planning a mission to Mars. He wants to build a base there, and perhaps one day a city.

Masterful millionaire

Elon wanted to use his money to tackle really big ideas. He founded the company SpaceX to build space-travel technology.

Spacecraft require hugely powerful rockets to be launched into space. Such rockets are very expensive to build, and most can only be used once! Elon decided to build reusable rockets, which could make space travel cheaper.

On 6 February 2018, his *Falcon Heavy* rocket lifted off with the help of 27 engines. It carried with it a red sportscar, which it took away from Earth's gravity and into orbit around the Sun. More importantly, the boosters from *Falcon Heavy* returned to Earth safely for reuse. Elon has big

plans for SpaceX, including building a base on Mars.

Elon has also turned his hand to Earth-travel. His company, Tesla, produces cars that use electricity instead of fossil fuels that pollute the environment. Another of Elon's ideas is the Hyperloop — a seated tube for transporting people or things extremely quickly. He plans for it to reach sensational speeds of around 1,300 kph (760 mph).

Elon has had many more ideas than would fit on these pages, and he'll probably have even more after this is written.

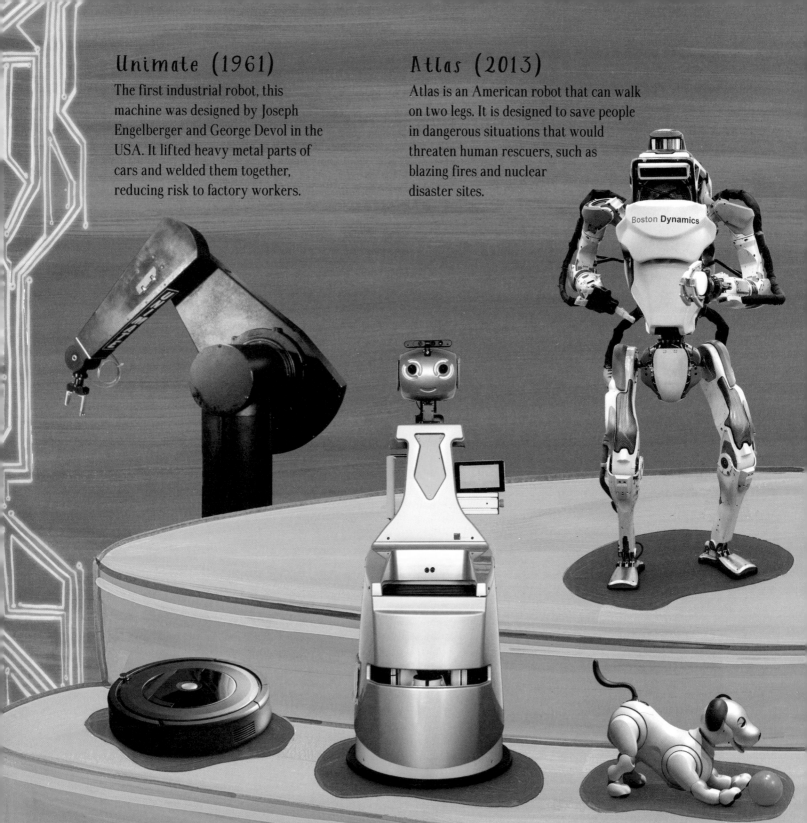

Unimate (1961)

The first industrial robot, this machine was designed by Joseph Engelberger and George Devol in the USA. It lifted heavy metal parts of cars and welded them together, reducing risk to factory workers.

Atlas (2013)

Atlas is an American robot that can walk on two legs. It is designed to save people in dangerous situations that would threaten human rescuers, such as blazing fires and nuclear disaster sites.

Vacuum cleaner

This little home robot makes housework fun. It is an automatic vacuum cleaner that rolls around cleaning the floor, avoiding furniture.

Robot-Era (2015)

This robot was trialled in an Italian nursing home to help care for elderly residents. It can ask simple questions, take blood pressure, and dispense drugs.

Aibo (2017)

Sony's robot dog is more than a toy – it's a friendly pet. It can recognize people, wag its tail, respond to commands, and eat artificial food.

Pepper (2014)

This Japanese humanoid robot conducts conversations and can recognise faces and human emotions. It was designed to be a companion in the home, and has also been used to help customers in shops, hotels, and banks.

ROBOTS

Humans have always been fascinated by robots. There are accounts of machines in ancient China that could serve food and play instruments. Modern robots are programmed to perform many tasks — they clean homes, police streets, and even photograph other planets. They range from industrial robots that work in factories to humanoid robots designed to interact with people.

Drones

Drones are pilotless aircraft, operated remotely, that were first developed during World War I. They are widely used in film-making, to carry goods, and by the police and military. People also fly them for fun.

Curiosity (2011)

Robots are needed for space exploration, as they can go to places where humans cannot survive. The Curiosity rover explores Mars and takes photographs that allow us to study its surface. It also samples chemicals and detects hazards, sending messages back to Earth.

Knightscope (2017)

Crime-fighting robots may seem like something from science fiction, but this robot was invented to help enforce the law in California, USA. It can recognize car number plates and detect moving objects.

MORE INVENTORS

Mary Anderson
1866–1953

When she was travelling from Alabama to New York City, Mary noticed that drivers kept having to stop to clear their windscreens of snow and ice. She invented the windscreen wiper, which is now a standard part of all cars around the world.

Maria Beasley
1847–1904

This American entrepreneur made a small fortune from her barrel-making invention. She also designed new and improved lifeboats that were used on the RMS *Titanic*, and saved 706 lives when the ship sank in 1912.

Enric Bernat
1923–2003

We have Enric to thank for inventing a popular sweet treat – the lollipop. This Catalan businessman saw that sweets made children's hands sticky, and had the bright idea to put them on sticks. He founded a company called Chupa Chups.

Shankar Abaji Bhise
1867–1935

Shankar was an Indian inventor responsible for hundreds of devices. His most significant invention was the Bhisotype. This machine quickly and cheaply produced the metal type used to print letters and symbols in books and newspapers.

Frances Gabe
1915–2016

This quirky American inventor hated housework so much that she developed a self-cleaning house, and even lived in it! Her patent included 68 inventions inside the house, such as a cupboard dishwasher and a self-cleaning bathtub.

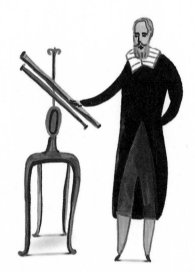

Galileo Galilei
1564–1642

This brilliant Italian astronomer was also an inventor. In 1609, he made a telescope that could magnify objects 20 times. While he was using it, Galileo discovered four of Jupiter's moons, and observed the phases of Venus.

Simone Giertz
1990–present

This Swedish inventor builds mechanical robots, and films them for her YouTube channel. Simone's robots are often not very practical, and fail in funny ways.

Guillermo González Camarena
1917–1965

Guillermo was a Mexican electrical engineer, and television pioneer. He developed several different colour television systems, and made the first colour television broadcast in Mexico.

László Biró
1899–1985

Born in Hungary, László invented the ballpoint pen, or biro. He wanted a pen with ink that dried quickly. The pen he created has a tiny ball in the tip that rolls around, leaving a line of ink on the paper. Billions of ballpoint pens are now made each year.

Xóchitl Guadalupe Cruz López
c.2010–present

Mexican inventor Xóchitl noticed that some families in her area couldn't afford to buy water heaters. She built a solar water heater using scrap materials. In 2018, she won an important science prize usually given to adults.

Benjamin Franklin
1706–1790

As well as being one of the Founding Fathers of the USA, Benjamin was a brilliant inventor and scientist. His inventions include a type of fireplace known as the Franklin stove, bifocal eyeglasses, and the lightning rod.

Arthur Fry
1931–present

This American inventor is responsible for a piece of stationery used in offices and homes around the world – the Post-it Note. Today, Arthur's sticky invention is sold in more than 100 countries.

Temple Grandin
1947–present

At the age of 18, Temple built a machine called a "hug box". This device is used to help calm people down, particularly those with disorders such as autism.

Margaret Hamilton
1936–present

Margaret is a trailblazing computer programmer. Working for NASA, she built the onboard flight software for the Apollo missions. Her work was essential to landing astronauts on the Moon for the first time.

Thérèse Izay Kirongozi
1973–present

Thérèse is an engineer from the Democratic Republic of Congo. She designed human-like robots to direct the traffic on the roads, in the hope of preventing unnecessary accidents.

George Klein
1904–1992

George invented, among other things, the first electric wheelchair, skis for aircraft, and a mechanical arm used on the Space Shuttle. This Canadian engineer is remembered as one of the most productive inventors of the 20th century.

Beth Koigi
c.1992–present

Beth is a Kenyan businesswoman who, along with Anastasia Kaschenko and Clare Sewell, invented a device that draws moisture from the air to produce clean drinking water.

Joseph-Michel & Jacques-Étienne Montgolfier
1740–1810 & 1745–1799

These French brothers were responsible for the hot-air balloon. The first human-piloted flight of one of their balloons took place in 1783, and the balloon travelled 3 km (2 miles).

Kary Mullis
1944–2019

American scientist Kary invented a technique for copying strands of DNA – the molecule inside cells that contains the code for life. The technique, known as PCR, earned him a Nobel Prize and revolutionized molecular biology.

Isaac Newton
1642–1727

As well as his famous work on gravity (inspired by a falling apple), Isaac invented the first practical reflecting telescope. It was smaller and more powerful than existing telescopes. He also created a branch of mathematics called calculus.

Seema Prakash
1961–present

Indian scientist Seema developed a highly successful and cheap way of making copies, or clones, of the best crops. She has taught her technique free of charge to many farmers in rural parts of India.

Boyan Slat
1994–present

Aged 16, this Dutch whizz-kid invented a way to harness the power of ocean currents to remove plastic from water. Boyan founded The Ocean Cleanup, an organization with the mission of developing technology to this end.

George Stephenson
1781–1848

This British engineer is called "The Father of Railways" for his pioneering work on rail transport. With his son, Robert, George built the first steam locomotive that powered a train carrying passengers on a public railway.

Alan Turing
1912–1954

This British mathematician developed a machine to break secret German codes during World War II. This helped the Allies (UK, USA, Soviet Union, and many other countries) win the war. Later, he did pioneering work in artificial intelligence (intelligence shown by machines).

Jane Ní Dhulchaointigh
c.1981–present

Jane is an Irish artist who invented a special type of glue called Sugru. It can be moulded into different shapes and used to repair all sorts of broken objects, from pull tabs on zips, to wellies.

Nicéphore Niépce
1765–1833

Frenchman Nicéphore took the first-ever permanent photograph using a type of camera called a "camera obscura" and a chemical called bitumen. It took eight hours to take the picture, but paved the way for better, faster cameras.

Louis Pasteur
1822–1895

One of the most famous French people ever, Louis invented a method to heat foods and drinks, killing off any germs in them so that they last longer. He also came up with other discoveries, including a way of protecting people against the infection rabies.

Anna Pavlova
1881–1931

Anna was a Russian ballerina who invented the modern *pointe* shoe worn by ballet dancers today. This shoe allows dancers to more easily stand on the tips of their toes. Anna performed all over the world, including South America, India, and the UK.

Mary Van Brittan Brown
1922–1999

This African-American nurse invented a home-security system with her husband. It had lots of features used in security systems today, such as cameras that allow the person inside to see who is at the door.

Jeanne Villepreux–Power
1794–1871

If you have a fish tank in your home, you should be grateful to this Frenchwoman. Jeanne created the first aquarium to observe and study sea creatures. She also made a wedding dress for a princess!

James Watt
1736–1819

This Scottish engineer invented the modern steam engine, which helped to spark the Industrial Revolution. This was a time when lots of big factories opened to produce goods, powered by James' engine, and many people moved to the cities for work.

Yuan Longping
1930–present

Longping, a Chinese farming expert, invented hybrid rice, which is a mixture of two varieties. This hybrid produced a bigger crop than other types of rice plant. Longping's rice is now grown around the world, helping to feed people in areas suffering from famine.

GLOSSARY

apprentice
Someone learning the skills of a trade, often working for little money for a few years until qualified

architect
Someone who designs buildings

artificial
Used to describe something that does not occur in nature or that is made by humans

astronomy
Study of the Universe beyond Earth, including the Solar System and galaxies

automobile
Another word for car

biology
Branch of science concerned with life and living things

Bluetooth
Technology that lets devices connect and share data wirelessly within a short range

Braille
System of raised dots for blind people to read using their sense of touch

chemistry
Branch of science concerned with substances and how they react with each other

climate change
Change in Earth's temperature and weather patterns that may be natural or caused by human activity

computer coding
Instructions, written in various computer languages, for computers and programs

courtier
Someone, usually of noble birth, who spent time at the court of a king or queen

degree (academic)
Award given for completing a course at university

density
The amount of mass, or matter, in a particular volume

element
Simplest substance with one type of atom (tiny particle). There are more than 100 different elements and they include hydrogen, carbon, oxygen, and gold

engineer
Someone who designs, makes, or looks after engines, machines, or buildings and other structures

entrepreneur
Someone who starts their own business

fossil fuel
Fuel made from plants and animals that died millions of years ago. Fossil fuels include gas, oil, and coal

generator
Device that generates electricity from other forms of energy

global warming
Rise in temperature all around the world. Global warming has increased due to humans burning fossil fuels, which raise the amount of gases such as carbon dioxide in the atmosphere

gravity
Invisible force of attraction between two objects, such as the pull between Earth and the Moon

Industrial Revolution
Period in history that started in the 18th century when machines were invented to produce goods in factories

International Space Station
Large space station and laboratory that orbits Earth. Often shortened to ISS

Internet
Communication network that links together computers all over the world

laboratory
Room in which scientific experiments are performed. Often shortened to lab

literacy
Ability to read and write

locomotive
Front part of a train that provides the power to pull the rest of it

magnetic
Used to describe magnets, which are objects that attract some substances, such as the metal iron, with an invisible force

mill
Factory containing machinery to make particular goods, such as cloth

molecule
Two or more atoms (tiny particles of a chemical element) bonded together

motor
Machine that powers a vehicle or another device with moving parts

NASA
US government agency responsible for space missions and space-related research. Short for National Aeronautic and Space Administration

naturalist
Someone who likes to observe or study living things in their natural environment

patent
Official document giving someone the right to make, use, or sell an invention

pharmacist
Someone who prepares and provides medicinal drugs

physics
Branch of science concerned with matter, movement, forces, and energy

prejudice
Judgement or opinion made before examining the facts

radiation
Movement of energy in the form of waves or particles. Sunlight, X-rays, and radio waves are all types of radiation. Some types can be harmful to living things

recycling
Using something old to make something new

renewable energy
Energy taken from sources that will not run out, such as sunlight, wind, and waves, to generate electricity. Also called green energy

robot
Moving machine that is programmed to do different tasks

satellite
Any object that travels around a planet, often made by humans to collect scientific information

solar power
Energy from sunlight that is converted into electricity for human use

suffragette
Woman who fought for suffrage – the right to vote – for women

time zone
Any of the 24 bands, running between the north and south poles, in which the same time is used

transplant
Medical operation in which a healthy part of a body is used to replace a diseased part

university
Place of higher education where students study for degrees

vial
Small container, usually glass, used for holding liquids

voltage
Force that makes tiny particles called electrons move in an electric current. Voltage is measured in volts (V)

Wi-Fi
Technology that lets phones, tablets, and computers connect to the Internet wirelessly

zoology
Study of animals

INDEX

About the author

Professor Robert Winston is a pioneer of successful medical techniques to treat couples who struggle to have children. A familiar face on television, Robert is also a member of the House of Lords, part of the UK Parliament. He has written and contributed to many DK children's STEAM books, including the prize-winning *Utterly Amazing Science*, *Home Lab*, *Science Squad*, and *Ask a Scientist*.

About the illustrator

Jessamy Hawke has been drawing since she was old enough to hold a pencil. She lives between London and Dorset, in the UK, where she enjoys walking along the coast and finding spots to sit and paint outdoors. Jessamy also illustrated *Explorers*, another DK children's book. When she's in the studio, she's kept company by her dog, Mortimer, and her two cats, Marcel and Rhubarb.

About the consultants

Dr Stephen Haddelsey is a British historian and the author of six books; he has also edited two historical manuscripts for their first publication. He is a Fellow of both the Royal Geographical Society and the Royal Historical Society.

Lisa Burke has been writing and consulting on science books for DK since 2005. She studied Natural Sciences at Cambridge University, then went on to work at Sky News as a presenter, weather forecaster, and science correspondent. She created the news platform RTL Today, and now lives in Luxembourg.

DK would like to thank: Jaileen Kaur and Vijay Kandwal for cut-outs; Emma Hobson and Eleanor Bates for design assistance; Steve Crozier for repro work; Caroline Hunt for proofreading; Helen Peters for the index; Ruth Amos, Olga D. González-Sanabria, Deepika Kurup, Yusuf Muhammad, Richard Turere, and Veena Sahajwalla for kindly agreeing to be interviewed and for providing images; Bianca Hezekiah for her insightful comments; Roohi Sehgal for advising on G. D. Naidu; and Eunyi Choi for her help researching Sejong the Great.

Picture Credits

The publisher would like to thank the following for their kind permission to reproduce their photographs:

(Key: a-above; b-below/bottom; c-centre; f-far; l-left; r-right; t-top)

8 Alamy Stock Photo: Everett Collection Inc (tr); Sowa Sergiusz (cra). Dorling Kindersley: Musee du Louvre, Paris (cb). 9 Alamy Stock Photo: Granger Historical Picture Archive (t); World History Archive (clb). Dorling Kindersley: © The Trustees of the British Museum. All rights reserved. (cra). 10 Alamy Stock Photo: Pictorial Press Ltd (cla). 11 Alamy Stock Photo: RGB Ventures / SuperStock (b). 12 Alamy Stock Photo: Universal Images Group North America LLC (cb). Dorling Kindersley: Jonathan Sneath (clb). Science & Society Picture Library: Science Museum (cla). 12-13 Getty Images: Science & Society Picture Library (bc). 13 Alamy Stock Photo: BRAZIL Landmarks and People by Vision (c); Science History Images (tr). Getty Images: ullstein bild (crb). 14 Alamy Stock Photo: Pictorial Press Ltd (tl). Getty Images: Science & Society Picture Library (clb). 15 Alamy Stock Photo: Chronicle (clb); The Print Collector (br). 16 Alamy Stock Photo: Science History Images (bc). Mercedes-Benz Classic: (cr). 17 Alamy Stock Photo: Historic Collection (cla); Tom Wood (tc). 18 Alamy Stock Photo: INTERFOTO (tl); Pictorial Press Ltd (bl). 19 Dreamstime.com: Johannes Gerhardus Swanepoel (br). Getty Images: Leemage / Universal Images Group (tr). 20 G D Naidu Charities, Coimbatore (TN): (tl, bl); 21 G D Naidu Charities, Coimbatore (TN): (tl, cra, br). 22 Getty Images: The Asahi Shimbun (tl). 23 Alamy Stock Photo: Newscom (br). 24 Alamy Stock Photo: SilverScreen (br). Getty Images: Robert Coburn / John Kobal Foundation (tr). 27 Alamy Stock Photo: Popperfoto (tr). NASA: (br). 28 Alamy Stock Photo: Everett Collection Inc (crb). Dorling Kindersley: The Science Museum, London (tr); Whipple Museum of History of Science, Cambridge (bl). 29 Alamy Stock Photo: Everett Collection Historical (tc); Granger Historical Picture Archive (bc). 32 Bridgeman Images: Pictures from History (cla). Dreamstime.com: Joymsk (bl). 33 Alamy Stock Photo: SIRIOH Co., LTD (cra). Dreamstime.com: Olga Khoroshunova (tl); Iuliia Nedrygailova (crb). 34 Alamy Stock Photo: Oldtime (br). Getty Images: Apic (tr). The Picture Art Collection (r); ZUMA Press, Inc. (br). 36 Alamy Stock Photo: Granger Historical Picture Archive (tr). Getty Images: Bettmann (cr). Science Photo Library: Miriam And Ira D. Wallach Division Of Art, Prints And Photographs / New York Public Library (bl). 37 Division of Work and Industry, National Museum of American History, Smithsonian Institution: (cra). Getty Images: maja / a.collectionRF (tr). 38 Getty Images: Bettmann (tl); Science & Society Picture Library (cr); Hulton Archive (crb). 39 Alamy Stock Photo: Björn Wylezich (cl). Getty Images: Hulton Archive (tl); Time Life Pictures / Mansell / The LIFE Picture Collection (br). 40 Alamy Stock Photo: GL Archive (tl). 42 Alamy Stock Photo: Archive PL (tr). 43 Getty Images: Bettmann (tr, cl). 44 Science Photo

Library: Dan Bernstein (tr). 45 Alamy Stock Photo: Everett Collection Inc (cra). Getty Images: Keystone (br). Press Association Images: Fiona Hanson / PA Archive (tl). 46 Science Photo Library: Hagley Museum And Archive (tl). 47 Alamy Stock Photo: Victor Nikitin (crb); Zoonar GmbH (br). Science Photo Library: Sinclair Stammers (tr). 48 Getty Images: Bettmann (tr); Juan Naharro Gimenez (tl). 49 Getty Images: Chip Somodevilla (cr). 50 Alamy Stock Photo: Ye Pingfan / Xinhua (tr). 51 Alamy Stock Photo: Manfred Ruckszio (br); Finnbarr Webster (cra). 52 Getty Images: Jemal Countess (tl). 54 Getty Images: Apic (clb); Time Life Pictures / Pix Inc. / The LIFE Picture Collection (cl). 56 Anna Kucera: Veena Sahajwalla (tr). 57 Getty Images: Matt King (cla). SMaRT Centre @ UNSW Sydney: Veena Sahajwalla (br). 58 Yusuf Muhammad: Dr Liman Muhammad (tl). 59 Yusuf Muhammad. 60 Getty Images: Lucas Oleniuk / Toronto Star (tr); Paul Treadway / Barcroft Media (clb). 61 Alamy Stock Photo: © Netflix - BBC Films - BFI Film Fund - Lipsync Post - Participant Media - Potboiler Productions / DR / TCD / Prod.DB (tc). 62 Ruth Amos: (tc). 63 Ruth Amos: Kids Invent Stuff ltd (cla). 64 Deepika Kurup: (tr, cr). 65 Deepika Kurup: (cl). 66 Lion lights: Richard Turere (tc, br). 67 Dreamstime. com: Sjors737 (br). Lion lights: Richard Turere (cla). 70 Alamy Stock Photo: Science History Images (br). Getty Images: Bettmann (tr). 71 Alamy Stock Photo: Chronicle (cra); GL Archive (tl). Getty Images: Science & Society Picture Library (cb). 72 Alamy Stock Photo: ART Collection (tr). Getty Images: DEA Picture Library (cla). 73 Alamy Stock Photo: Art Collection 3 (tr). 74 Alamy Stock Photo: Granger Historical Picture Archive (tl, br). 75 Dreamstime.com: Kenneth Vaughn (br). 76 Alamy Stock Photo: Heritage Image Partnership Ltd (tl). Getty Images: Science & Society Picture Library (bl). 77 Getty Images: Photo Josse / Leemage / Corbis (cr). 78 Dreamstime. com: Georgios Kollidas (tr). 79 Alamy Stock Photo: Chronicle (c); Science History Images (cla). Getty Images: Science & Society Picture Library (br). 80 Alamy Stock Photo: Matthew Brady / Pictorial Press Ltd (tl, b). 81 Alamy Stock Photo: agefotostock (tr). 82 Wikipedia: Sarah Elisabeth Goode (tc). 83 Alamy Stock Photo: Sergio Azenha (cr). Dreamstime.com: Denisismagilov (tr). 84 123RF. com: ljupco (c). 85 Dreamstime.com: Sergey Mostovoy (tl); Supertrooper (cl); Pioneer111 (cr). iStockphoto.com: Marcelo Trad (cr). 86 Getty Images: Hulton Archive (tr). 86-87 Getty Images: Bettmann (bc). 87 Alamy Stock Photo: Granger Historical Picture Archive (tl); northshoot - Food (tl). 88 Alamy Stock Photo: Everett Collection Historical (bl); PF-(usna) (cra). 89 Alamy Stock Photo: Science History Images (cra). 90 Dreamstime.com: Edgars Sermulis (cr); Toxitz (crb). 91 Dreamstime. com: Alexlmx (cb); Kari Høglund / Karidesign (tl); Ilfede (tc); Vudhikul Ocharoen (clb); Aprescindere / Rubik's Cube® used by permission of Rubik's Brand Ltd www.rubiks. com (c). 92 Alamy Stock Photo: agefotostock (cb). 93 Alamy Stock Photo: GL Archive (br). Getty Images: Smith Collection / Gado (tr). 94 Alamy Stock Photo: Archive Pics (tl). Getty Images: © Hulton-Deutsch Collection / CORBIS (cra). 95 Alamy Stock Photo: INTERFOTO (bl). Getty Images: Science & Society Picture Library (tr). 98 Alamy Stock Photo: Chronicle (tl). 99 Alamy Stock

Photo: Holger Hollemann / dpa picture alliance archive (bc). 100-101 123RF. com: millions27 (bc). 101 Getty Images: Science & Society Picture Library (cr). 102 Dorling Kindersley: Barnabas Kindersley (l). Science Photo Library: Martyn F. Chillmaid (bc). 104 Alamy Stock Photo: Aclosund Historic (tl); ART Collection (cl); Istanbul Jazari Museum (clb). 106 Alamy Stock Photo: Pictorial Press Ltd (tl); Sirioh Co., Ltd (bl). 107 Alamy Stock Photo: Xinhua (tr). 108 Alamy Stock Photo: North Wind Picture Archives (crb). 109 Alamy Stock Photo: Mark Summerfield (tc). 110 Alamy Stock Photo: The Granger Collection (tl); Roberto Herrett (cra). Getty Images: Science & Society Picture Library (bc). 111 Alamy Stock Photo: ART Collection (cra); IanDagnall Computing (tl). Bridgeman Images: British Library Board. All Rights Reserved (cr). 112 Getty Images: Science & Society Picture Library (bl). 113 Alamy Stock Photo: Tango Images (tc). Dreamstime.com: Ariwasabi (br). 114 Alamy Stock Photo: GL Archive (tl); World History Archive (br). 115 Alamy Stock Photo: INTERFOTO (tc, crb); Akademie / The Nobel Prize Medal is a registered trademark of the Nobel Foundation (br). 116 Alamy Stock Photo: Rimus (cb); Russell (c). Getty Images: Ken Faught / Toronto Star (crb). Science Photo Library: Royal Institution Of Great Britain (bl). 117 Alamy Stock Photo: WENN Rights Ltd (bc). Dreamstime.com: Pavel Losevsky (tl). Getty Images: Michael Stuparyk / Toronto Star (cl); Meurisse / ullstein bild Dtl. (cra). iStockphoto. com: Andreas Kermann (tl). 118 Library of Congress, Washington, D.C.: Hine, Lewis Wickes, 1874-1940 / National Child Labor Committee collection (tr, cra). 118-119 Division of Work and Industry, National Museum of American History, Smithsonian Institution: (bc). 119 Photo Scala, Florence: © 2020 Digital image, The Museum of Modern Art, New York (br). 120 Science Photo Library: Sheila Terry (tl). 121 Alamy Stock Photo: Chronicle (br). ©Imperial War Museum: (FEQ 846) (cr). 122 Alamy Stock Photo: IanDagnall Computing (tl). Getty Images: Science & Society Picture Library (bc). 123 Alamy Stock Photo: Everett Collection Historical (tl); Tango Images (cr). 124 Science Photo Library: Emilio Segre Visual Archives / American Institute Of Physics (cl). 125 Alamy Stock Photo: Arco Images GmbH (cr). Getty Images: Hulton Archive (bc). 127 Getty Images: Bettmann (tr); Keystone (clb). 128 Getty Images: Karjean Levine (cla). 129 Getty Images: Science & Society Picture Library (tc). 130 Olga D. González-Sanabria: (tl). 130-131 NASA: (tc). 131 NASA: Johnson Space Centre (cr). 132 Alamy Stock Photo: NASA Photo (bl). Dreamstime.com: Oleg07871 (cla). Getty Images: David Becker (ca); Matt Stroshane (tr). 134 Alamy Stock Photo: Granger Historical Picture Archive (cl). Dreamstime.com: Hakinmhan (clb). Getty Images: The Asahi Shimbun (crb); Laura Lezza (c); Kiyoshi Ota / Bloomberg (cr). 135 Dreamstime.com: Viktor Birkus (c). Getty Images: Junko Kimura-Matsumoto / Bloomberg (cl); Rob Lever / AFP (clb). NASA: JPL-Caltech (crb)

All other images © Dorling Kindersley
For further information see: www.dkimages.com